The Great Gasbag

Also by Joy Behar

*Joy Shtick: Or What Is the Existential Vacuum and
Does It Come with Attachments?*

*When You Need a Lift: But Don't Want to Eat
Chocolate, Pay a Shrink, or Drink a Bottle of Gin*

An A-*to*-Z Study Guide to Surviving Trump World

JOY BEHAR

The Great Gasbag

HARPER

An Imprint of HarperCollins*Publishers*

HarperCollins books may be purchased for educational, business, or sales promotional use. For information, please email the Special Markets Department at SPsales@harpercollins.com.

FIRST EDITION

Designed by Bonni Leon-Berman

Library of Congress Cataloging-in-Publication Data has been applied for.

ISBN 978-0-06-269934-3

17 18 19 20 21   LSC   10 9 8 7 6 5 4 3 2 1

Dedicated to the

65,853,216

American

voters

who knew

better.

Author's Note

In 2015, when the presidential campaigns first began, my agent called me begging, *begging* me to write a political book. I told him I was too busy. Then he called my manager and started begging him to get me to write a book. He, too, told him I was busy. Then he called my husband, who slept through the call. Ditto, my daughter. Then the sly puss called my brilliant (then-four-year-old) grandson, who took the call. But the kid was slyer than he was. He told him, "My nana's a busy woman. She's on TV every day, she does live performances and occasional film work; she doesn't have time to write a book. But I'll tell you what, if something really weird happens, like that crazy guy with the orange face wins, call us back."

Well, on November 9, 2016, the day after the election, my phone rang again. I didn't need to be begged. I didn't even need to be asked. By the time I woke up that morning, the horror of what happened the night before had already sunk in. When I looked in the bathroom mirror, instead of seeing the gorgeous punim you all see on TV every day looking back at me, I saw Edvard Munch's *The Scream*. It was time to put pen to paper.

But what to write? Given the mercurial nature of Trump and the chaos of his campaign, I knew I couldn't write a traditional book, because in Trump World, like in the Emerald City of Oz, "things around here change so quickly" that if I wrote something in the morning, it might be out of date by dinnertime.

In fact, despite all due diligence and with an eye on timeliness, I'm pretty sure that by the time you read this, some of the people I've written about will have: been fired (Sean Spicer), been reassigned (Kellyanne Conway), left the country (Melania), been jailed (General Flynn), or moved to a kibbutz in Israel (the Kushners).

What to write came to me quite by coincidence. I was sitting in a Starbucks across from *The View* studio one day, on the Upper West Side of Manhattan, when I overheard a man and a woman talking. (And by "overheard," I mean I was eavesdropping.) Since 83 percent of the people in that neighborhood are psychiatrists, psychologists, therapists, or social workers, I thought their conversation would be worth "overhearing." The woman said, "I saw an accident on Eighty-Sixth Street this morning." The man replied, "You wanna talk about accidents? Trump has the nuclear codes. He might accidentally set off a missile. So, what happened on Eighty-Sixth Street?" The woman answered, "A taxi ran a red light and hit a pole." And the man said, "You wanna talk red? Trump's in bed with the Russians! How's that for red?"

It was like word association. Suddenly, it dawned on me—Dr. Freud and the woman with the decaf latte gave me the concept for this book: an alphabetical guide to Trump World.

It's perfect for me; I used to be a New York City public school teacher. (I taught delinquents the difference between *who* and *whom*.)

So, now that I knew what the book was, I had to figure out what to call it. Choosing a title for a book is almost as important as the book itself, because if the fifteen words on the cover don't work, nobody will read the fifty thousand words inside. Think about it——If *Uncle Tom's Cabin* had been called *Uncle Tom's Condo*, do you think it would have become an American classic? Would Harriet Beecher Stowe have gotten a three-book deal and a TV movie offer from Lifetime? No. *Green Eggs and Ham* made Dr. Seuss a literary giant. I don't think *Egg White Omelet and Chicken* would have even put him on the map.

Needless to say, a lot of thought went into choosing the title for this book. I knew it was going to be subtitled *An A-to-Z Study Guide to Surviving Trump World*, but I wanted the main title to be both clever and on point. And since I'm a fan of the classics, that's where I started. Here are some other titles I considered before deciding on *The Great Gasbag*:

> *Moby Dickhead*
> *Con with the Wind*
> *Pride and Very Prejudiced*
> *Catcher in the Lie*
> *Not Such Great Expectations*
> *The Age of Ignorance*
> *Gullible's Travels*
> *A Farewell to the Constitution*
> *The Son-in-Law Also Rises*
> *War and Hairpiece*

Maybe I'll use one of those titles for the follow-up book. We'll see. Anyway, I hope you have as much fun reading this as

I did writing it. (And by "fun," I mean the catharsis of writing saved me a fortune in therapy bills.)

Happy reading!
Joy

P.S. My agent didn't actually beg me to write this book. That's an "alternative fact," something you can read about in the *A*s.

[Disclaimer]

Dear ~~President Trump~~ (no, I can't bring myself to do it)

Dear ~~Mr. President~~ (same thing, ucch)

Dear ~~Donald,~~ (even though I was at one of his weddings, it feels too informal)

Dear ~~Orange Devil~~ (too much, too soon)

Dear Mr. Trump (boring, but whatever),

First, let me say that I don't imagine you'll read this book because I know you're way too busy watching TV and tweeting, and also because it's not written in Russian. I also know that you have thin skin and don't react well to jokes made at your expense, so on the off chance that Kellyanne or Ivanka tells you about it, please note that *The Great Gasbag* is satire, a protected literary genre, and that I, Joy Behar, am a satirist. If you don't believe me, ask my fifth-grade teacher, Mrs. Pellegra, who called me the "Jonathan Swift of P.S. 168." (I don't know where Mrs. Pellegra is these days, but Mount Carmel Cemetery might be a good place to start looking.)

The definition of *satire* is:

A genre of literature . . . in which vices, follies, abuses, and shortcomings are held up to ridicule, ideally with the intent of shaming individuals, corporations, government, or society itself into improvement. Although satire is usually meant to be humorous, its greater purpose is often constructive social criticism, using wit to draw attention to both particular and wider issues in society.[1]

Notice how it says satire is used as a tool to improve things? That's important, not just because it explains intent, but because it means that in addition to my being a comedian, talk show host, and satirist, I'm also a giver. And if you don't believe me, ask my old Girl Scout troop leader, Mrs. Defazio. (I don't know where she is these days, but you can probably get her number from Mrs. Pellegra.)

Happy reading!
Joy

[1]   Robert C. Elliott, "The Nature of Satire," *Encyclopedia Britannica*, 2004.

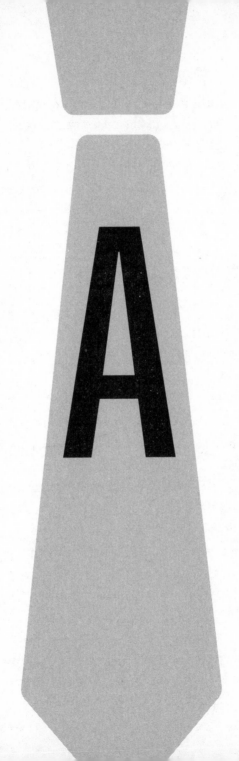

A **is for Acid Reflux.** Which is what 65,853,216 Americans get every time Trump holds a televised pep rally or press conference. Last week I had some friends over to my house for supper. Just as we sat down, The Donald came on TV, and all of a sudden eight stomachs rumbled and roared simultaneously—it was like listening to the flatulence scene in *Blazing Saddles*. Within two seconds of Orangeface showing up on-screen, my friends were yelling, "Gino, I'm gassy," and "Angie, the sausage and peppers are coming up." And they hadn't even eaten yet!

A **is for Alimony.** I have not seen the paperwork on any of Donald's divorces, but I'll bet he's spending a lot more on Valentine's Day gifts for Vladimir Putin than he is on alimony for Ivana and Marla combined.

A **is for All's Noisy on the Western Front**. Remember how nice and quiet things were before November 8, 2016? No chaos, no crazy, no wall-to-wall havoc. For sixteen years, the country was pretty much scandal-free. Other than George W. Bush invading the wrong country and Dick Cheney shooting his BFF in the face, things were calm. The only "scandal" No Drama Obama faced was the "birther" idiocy, which was just racist nonsense created by Trump. But since The Donald took over, we've had more noise and commotion than a Lamaze class at the Duggars' house.

A **is for Alternative Facts.** *Alternative facts* is an oxymoron, like *diet soda, deafening silence,* and *President Trump*. Alternative facts are lies. I prefer *lies* because "Alternative-facter, alternative facter, pants on fire," offends the Maya Angelou in me.

Some little white lies are acceptable. For example, whenever you're asked, "Does this dress make me look fat?" the answer is always, "No." (Especially if the person asking is J. Edgar Hoover.) Another example of when it's okay to lie: Last week, my grandson asked me, "Nana, how come Arnold Schwarzenegger's housekeeper's son can lift a couch over his head? And why does he have an Austrian accent?" Because my grandson is only six, and I was too exhausted that day to launch into a discussion of DNA, I simply said, "Your Mommy's on the phone; she says she wants to buy you some brand-new toys and give you one hundred dollars!" Was that wrong of me?

Trump's spokespeople are savvy enough not to own the lies themselves, so they pin them on him—and he's not smart enough to know they're doing it. Instead of saying that the president is actually lying or using alternative facts, they simply say, "The president believes . . . ," which

A is for **Alternative facts.** Alternative facts are *lies.* I prefer lies because "Alternative-facter, alternative facter, pants on fire," offends the Maya Angelou in me.

gets them off the hook for his particular brand of insanity. We've all heard his flacks say, "The president believes that three to five million illegal ballots were cast for Hillary Clinton, which cost him the popular vote," and "The president believes that Barack Obama was born in Kenya." Or, "The president believes Obama wiretapped his apartment in Trump Tower," or, "The president believes Paul Manafort had nothing whatsoever to do with Trump's presidential campaign." But those aren't the only alternative facts The Donald takes to heart. There are others.

I have a lot of friends in Washington, DC, so I did a little digging. And by "digging," I mean I got them drunk and taped our conversations without their permission. And in their vodka-induced stupors, they blabbed a lot of other ridiculous things the president believes:

- Melania married him for his looks.

- Andrea Bocelli is not really blind. He only pretends to be just to beat the rigged system and get handicapped parking spots.

- Meryl Streep is a mullah from Afghanistan. And she's an over-rated mullah.

- Melania married him for his sexual prowess.

- Barbra Streisand, Madonna, Adele, Justin Bieber, Tony Bennett, Bruce Springsteen, Fleetwood Mac, Sam Cooke, Frank Sinatra, Dean Martin, and Billie Holiday sang "great" at his inauguration.

- Melania married him for his giant hands.

- Corinthians II was better than Corinthians III but not as good as the original Corinthians, or even the fine Corinthian leather in his Dodge convertible.

- Voter fraud in the 2016 election was so rampant that Vladimir Putin was cheated out of being the junior senator from the great state of New York.

- Sasha and Malia are two-thirds of the defunct singing group Destiny's Child. And Beyoncé got out because she was jealous of their Secret Service protection.

- China made Mexico pay for the Great Wall.

- Marla Maples married him for his looks.

- NASA owes him fifty million dollars because Neil Armstrong planted the flag on a plot of land on the moon that he owns.

- Angela Merkel would be a better leader if she had cheek implants and tighter abs.

- His wives Ivana and Melania were both born in Altoona, Pennsylvania. And they both speak perfect English without a trace of an accent.

- The Statue of Liberty should produce a birth certificate or be deported back to France.

- America's children are not obese; the media is using special cameras to make kids look fat, just to hurt food companies.

- Marla Maples married him because of his sexual prowess.

- We should take sand from Iraq because it will be good for the terrarium industry.

- California is a foreign country, and he plans on invading it sometime between now and his next dye job.

- Marla Maples married him because of his giant hands.

- Mike Pence is a transgender bathroom attendant from Fond du Lac, Wisconsin.

- The two hundred thousand women who "marched" in Washington were actually just standing on line to get into the restaurant in his amazing, great, fabulous, super-duper, wowee-zowee hotel.

- The national anthem should be replaced with "I've Got to Be Me."

- The publishing industry is rigged against him because *The Diary of Anne Frank* sold more copies than *The Art of the Deal*. Donald feels *The Art of the Deal* is way more touching.

- His next wife will marry him because of his looks, sexual prowess, and giant hands.

A is for Anti-Choice. The A-word is the F-word of right-wing, Republican politics. It's more important than the B-word (*business*), the E-word (*education*), or the H-word (*health care*); the only word it's not more important than is the M-word (*money*).

Republicans believe that life begins at conception. If life does begin at conception, then my daughter was actually born on November 8 . . . or November 14, 22, or 27, or January 9. (I can't believe what a horny housewife I was back then.) And she was conceived either in my house; in a Motel 6 on Kissena Boulevard, Queens; or in a Chevrolet in the parking lot of a Motel 6 on Kissena Boulevard. My ex-husband spared no expense.

If life begins at conception, then everyone in this country is actually nine months older than it says on their driver's licenses. So, I guess millions of old people are owed billions of dollars in missing Social Security payments. Wouldn't it be easier to just say that life begins when you're old enough to get Botox and you're on your third marriage?

Ais for **Antidepressants.** Which is what 65,853,216 Americans started popping on November 9, 2016.

Ais for **Anxiety.** Ever since Election Night, when a journalist friend texted me, "Holy shit," which told me that the unthinkable was about to happen, I have been in a continuous state of high anxiety. Could it be that for the next four years, this bloviating incompetent would be in charge of the nuclear codes? Friends of mine—the ones who are *not* normally on Prozac—suddenly were contacting psychopharmacologists on the Internet for meds. Fortunately, I have a TV show on which to rant and rave on a daily basis, so I remained drug-free. Unfortunately, all my ranting and raving is not nearly enough. In order to inform future generations of the decline of democracy as we know it, one must put things in writing. Hopefully, when millennials and Generation Z read this (or listen to it on their headphones when they're at work writing code for a tech giant), they will go to the polls and vote with their heads and not write in "Teresa Giudice" or "Kanye" or whoever is the reality star of the day. Also, I need to exorcise the intense emotional upheaval being caused by this egomaniacal con man who thought best to kick off Sexual Assault Awareness Month by defending the since-fired serial harasser Bill O'Reilly, whose idea of foreplay is using a loofah as a sex toy. What do you expect from the grabber in chief?

A is for Appalled. Which is what my grandson was when Trump was announced the winner. The boy had a stunned look on his sweet, innocent little face, and he said, "Nana! What the fuck?"

A is for *The Apprentice.* Nothing says "qualified to be president" quite like being on a reality show. Why else is Omarosa sitting in the West Wing? I doubt The Donald would have appointed Rick Perry energy secretary if he hadn't first appeared on *Dancing with the Stars*. Poor Gary Busey was hoping to be head of the Food and Drug Administration, but they were afraid he would have a relapse and steal all the drugs. Donald should put the women from *Mob Wives* in there—at least they'd know how to handle Paul Ryan and Mitch McConnell. And Ramona would bitch-slap Trey Gowdy in a New York minute.

A is for Argentina. Or, as Steve Bannon and Steve Miller think of it, "our weekend getaway." And I do mean getaway!

A is for Arrested Development. Donald Trump is seventy but acts like he's seven. Forget the tantrums and name-calling and making faces. Every time he signs an executive order, he holds it up to show everyone. He's so proud of himself, like a boy who's pulled an ouchless Band-Aid off his knee without crying. Then he flashes this giant, fake, shit-eating grin. I'm not sure if he's smiling because he thinks it's a good executive order or because he's spelled his name right and stayed within the lines.

A is for the Arts. Donald Trump wants to defund the National Endowment for the Arts, probably because he hates anything that's more well-endowed than he is. Next year, he plans on getting rid of Ron Jeremy and all photos of Gary Cooper.

A is for Atlas. Atlas is Donald Trump's doppelganger. The Big A and the Orange D have some things in common: They both had lots of children with different wives, they both have the weight of the world on their shoulders, and they both think they're gods. The only differences are that (a) Atlas really had to carry the world on his shoulders as a punishment handed down by Zeus; Trump only *thinks* he has the weight of the world on his shoulders because he's a paranoid narcissist; and (b) Atlas never called his daughter a "piece of ass."

A **is for Authoritarian.** All the media types keep saying Trump has "authoritarian tendencies." I disagree. Sophia on *The Golden Girls* has authoritarian tendencies. The bitch who cut in front of me on line at Chico's has authoritarian tendencies. Trump is a bombastic blowhard and a bully. Now, would they please hide the nuclear codes from him? (Ivanka, you're in the White House. Sneak in and get the codes away from him. Do it while he's tweeting; he'll never notice.)

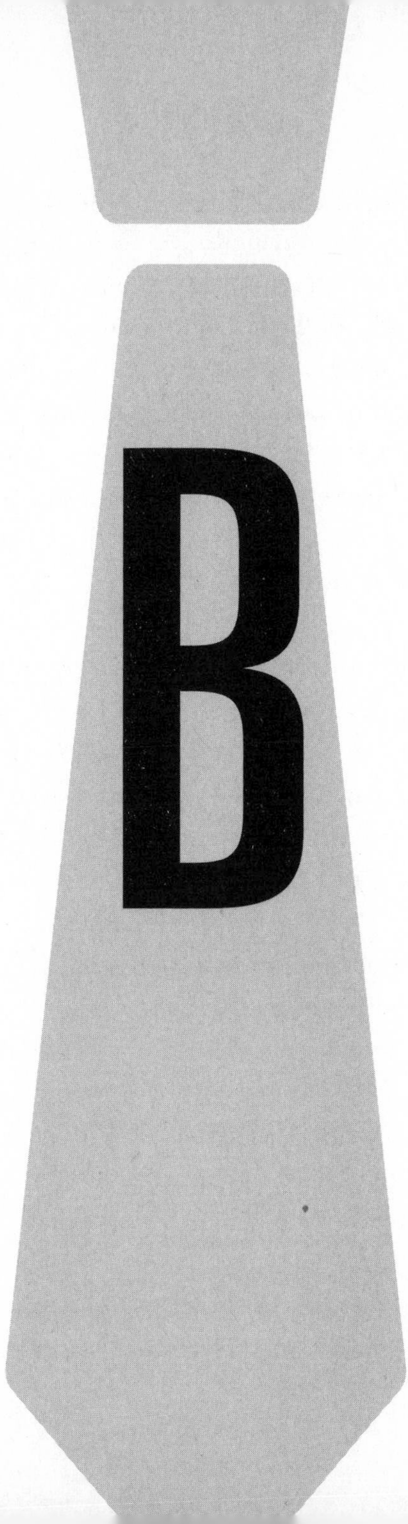
B

B **is for Bankruptcy.** Or, as Trump thinks of it, business as usual. Most people consider filing for bankruptcy a sad, traumatic, life-altering, devastating process. Donald Trump considers it "Tuesday." To be fair, The Donald has never declared personal bankruptcy—don't worry, the money he bilked you out of is safe and sound—but he *has* declared corporate bankruptcy *six times*. That's a lot. Think about it: George W. Bush allowed half of Lousiana to drown only that one time, Strom Thurmond sired only one black child, and Howard Taft got stuck in the White House bathtub only once.

B **is for Steve Bannon.** What you probably don't know is that Steve Bannon is the love child of Darth Vader and Leni Riefenstahl. For some odd reason, Trump listens to him. On a scale of one to painful rectal itch, Bannon's a nine. He basically wants to destroy democracy while making sure he has lots of money and power when it's all over.

Oh, wait. I'm wondering if the "odd reason" Trump listens to Bannon is because Bannon has pictures of Trump naked in a bubble bath with a goat, a rubber hose, and a blow-up doll named Cindy. It's possible.

B **is for Base (Trump's, that is).** Nick Kristof, the two-time Pulitzer Prize–winning columnist for the *New York Times*, says that we liberals should start a movement: We have to have more empathy toward Trump voters. We should be kinder, gentler progressives, like Bernie Bros on 'shrooms. But despite Kristof's plea, people on the left are still vicious about the

Trumpies. One woman tweeted to Kristof, "I absolutely despise these people. Truly the worst of humanity. To hell with every one of them." So much for bleeding heart liberals.

Me? I save that vitriol for the grabber in chief, Donald himself.

Having said that, I must say it's difficult to go all nicey-nicey Sarah McLachlan on some of these people, half of whom do not believe in evolution, global warming, or even that the earth is older than Larry King. Some of them have drunk the Trump Kool-Aid.

For example, Trump is okay with reintroducing pesticides into the environment, and his supporters are like, "Look, I don't have two heads and I grew up sprinkling DDT on my Cocoa Puffs." Fine, but when your granddaughter is her own twin and that "certain glow on her face" is uranium, don't come to me yelling, "What happened?"

How is reintroducing dangerous pesticides a good thing? That type of thing has to stop because I'm on this friggin' planet, too. Just because the Trumpies don't have a problem eating lettuce that has hands and feet, it doesn't mean no one else does.

As far as evolution goes, I don't really give a rat's ass what you believe, but don't start teaching creationism in my kid's school. Call me kookie, but I live in reality, and I can't say with a straight face that Noah actually had all those animals on one boat and they were paired up like they'd met on Tinder.

Many liberals think Trump voters are stupid. Be advised, we're not talking about *all* Trump voters. A lot of people who voted for Trump aren't mouth-breathing troglodytes. Many of them are probably normal(ish) and just voted for change, or because they always vote Republican, or because they'd had a three-way with Ann Coulter and Mitch McConnell. Whatever the reason, *they were conned*. No, it's the hard-core Trump base I have trouble cozying up to. I'm talking about the people who go from rally to rally waving Confederate flags, sporting swastika tattoos, and routinely punching people who've spelled their signs correctly.

B is for **Bankruptcy.** Or, as Trump thinks of it, business as usual. Most people consider filing for bankruptcy a sad, traumatic, life-altering, devastating process. Donald Trump considers it "Tuesday."

Liberals like to point out that a solid 47 percent of the Trump base thinks Frederick Douglass is still alive (and that Barbara Walters is dating him). I imagine the other 53 percent has no idea who Frederick Douglass was. But I can forgive that; I don't know everybody who fought for the slave states. But some of the other things they buy into defy logic. A lot of Trumpies still believe that Obama was born in Kenya (even after DT 'fessed up that those claims weren't true); many of them believe Obama was involved in 9/11 (even though he didn't become president until 2009); some of them actually believe Hillary Clinton used a body double to hide the fact she had Parkinson's, MS, and AIDS—at the same time. (For that to be true, her body double would have had to be David Blaine or both Penn *and* Teller.) When I hear such craziness, I shake my head and think, *What are these people smoking?*

But when I read that nearly half of them think that Black History Month should be counteracted with White History Month, I had to rethink the whole thing. First of all, it's White History Month every month, okay? So why would you need *one* month for it? Do these people not realize that if you choose one month for White History Month, then you are losing the other eleven? Okay, I'm calming down. I'm trying the Nick Kristof experiment.

B **is for Believe Me.** Whenever Trump says an outrageous or false thing, he usually follows it with the words "believe me." For example, "I'm going to defeat ISIS in my first thirty days. Believe me"; "I'm going to replace Obamacare with something great. Believe me"; "I may have small hands but there's no problem *down there*. Believe me." If you take away only one thing from this book, let it be "never believe someone when he says, 'Believe me.'"

Believe me.

B **is for Beriberi.** The only disease to be covered by the Republican health care plan. Beriberi is a thiamine-deficiency disease found almost exclusively on the island of Java. Which is why the plan covers it; no one in America gets beriberi.

B is for Bigly. Believe it or not, *bigly* is actually a word, but it's rarely used in English. Or French. Or Dutch. Or Spanish. Or even that click-click language they speak in parts of Africa. It's one of those words that you never use and avoid saying, like *obstreperous*, *antediluvian*, or *cunnilingus*. *Bigly* is an adverb meaning "largely or generously," two words rarely associated with Donald Trump. (Ironically, he uses it a lot.) There was a lot of conversation as to whether Trump was using *bigly* or was simply mispronouncing *big league*. Either way, it doesn't matter; it's not exactly soaring oratory.

B is for Blowhard. No, I'm not talking about fabulous gay weekends on Fire Island. I'm talking about nightmarish weekdays listening to Sean Hannity on the radio. Lots of media pundits have big mouths and rant and rave for ratings, but few of them have as little information as Sean Hannity. He's like an unfunny episode of *Seinfeld*: he's carrying on about nothing. Whenever I listen to him, which is when I'm trapped in a broken elevator or being held hostage in the trunk of Steven Mnuchin's car, I can't believe my ears—not just because of the paucity of facts, but because I don't know how he manages to speak so clearly with his lips attached to Trump's ass.

B is for Body Snatchers. At first blush, some of the people on Team Trump appear to be nice people, pleasant almost.

James Glover/Reuters

They seem like the kind of folks you could have a drink with or invite to the house for dinner and not have to worry about them stealing the silverware. But, upon closer inspection, you see that something is wrong with most of them, something very wrong. At first, you notice there's a slight tic or an uncomfortable hunch of the shoulders; then comes the frozen, vacant stare; and finally, the lies start spewing from their mouths like feral cats auditioning for one of those Meow Mix commercials. Then it dawns on you: this isn't just a White House press conference; it's the latest remake of *Invasion of the Body Snatchers*.

Before joining Team Trump as press secretary, Sean Spicer was a nice, albeit bland, man in ill-fitting suits. He's from Manhasset, Long Island. He has a degree in government, a wife, and two children, and he worked for the Republican National Committee. But then he got snatched up by one of the aliens from Team Trump and sucked into the pod factory of craziness. Shortly after being snatched, Spicer became a sweaty wreck, speaking in double-talk and lies, backtracking and spinning, all the while staring blankly into space. Sean, "Sleep . . . sleep . . . and be born again into a world without fear and hate!" Where's Donald Sutherland when you need him?

B **is for Breitbart News.** Another oxymoron. Breitbart has as much in common with news as Rush Limbaugh has with a twenty-four-hour fitness center. Andrew Breitbart founded the conservative website in 2007 as a platform for antiprogressive views. After Breitbart had the decency to die of a heart attack in 2012, Steve Bannon took over and declared the website a platform for the alt-right movement. Although Breitbart News is presently available in English, it's much more fun to read it out loud in a German accent.

The website is also known for its ridiculous conspiracy theories. Two of the most famous ones are that President Obama killed Supreme Court justice Antonin Scalia—his 2016 death was ruled to be from "natural causes": he was seventy-nine years old and obese—and that Obama orchestrated the "murders" of both Andrew Breitbart and, sixty days later, the doctor who performed his autopsy.

I can't wait for their next round of nonsensical theories. Maybe they'll claim that JFK's assassination was a suicide; or that Oprah is really a white Swedish boy named Anders; or that Liberace was straight.

B **is for Broke.** Really, really rich people never talk about how rich they are. Not once has the Sultan of Brunei ever called me to brag about the gazillion camels he owns. Which makes me think that The Donald doth proclaim too much. It's entirely possible that Trump may not be as rich as he says he is, which may be one of the reasons he won't release his tax returns. Maybe he is actually broke (in billionaire terms). He may be leveraged to the hilt and in debt up to his eyes. If that's true, how long do you think Melania will remain Mrs. Trump? I can't decide which would be more delicious, Donald not having money for health insurance right after he repeals the Affordable Care Act, or Donald living in a refrigerator box on the sidewalk in front of Trump Tower. Ahhh, a girl can dream.

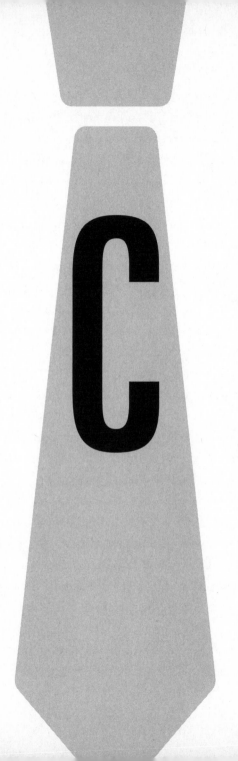

C is for Cabinet. One of Donald Trump's campaign slogans was "Drain the Swamp" (along with "Build the Wall," "Lock 'er Up," "Make America Great Again," and "Obama's from Kenya"). Turns out he did drain the swamp—right into his Cabinet. Most of his Cabinet appointments were (shockingly!) old, rich, well-connected white guys, although he made sure to appoint a rich, well-connected white woman and a minority or two, either as a personal favor (Elaine Chao, wife of Mitch McConnell) or as a sop to part of his base (Dr. Ben Carson, the love muffin of the evangelical "Christians"). With few exceptions, the one thing that his Cabinet members have in common is a total lack of experience in or knowledge of the departments they're heading.

Dr. Ben Carson was appointed the secretary of housing and urban development. Apparently, his qualification was that he lives in a house. When Ben Carson was running for the Republican nomination, he said some pretty wacky things: "Obamacare is the worst thing since slavery," "Prison turns people gay," and "Joseph built the pyramids to store grain." Republicans defended his kookiness by saying, "He must be smart. He's a doctor!" I don't see the connection, but next time my bursitis erupts, I'll make sure to call my plumber.

I think Republicans love Ben Carson because he loves Jesus—which makes me think that by the end of his term, instead of housing projects, he'll have everyone living in mangers.

Then there was Secretary of State Rex Tillerson, the Marcel Marceau of the Cabinet. The man never speaks. Reporters ask him questions, and he says nothing; he just smiles at them like a puppy who's being praised for peeing on the paper. All Rex needs is white face paint and a beret and he could stand on a street corner in Paris and pretend he's walking in the wind. What qualified him to be secretary of state? Why, nothing, of course—this is Trump World! Prior to joining the Cabinet, Tillerson was the CEO of ExxonMobil, the company known for record-high prices, consumer gouging, and the huge oil spill in Alaska in 1989. Remember that? The *Exxon Valdez* was an oil tanker that ran aground in 1989 and spilled hundreds of thousands of gallons of oil into Prince William Sound. As CEO, RexxonMobil spent almost twenty years in litigation trying to minimize paying for his company's negligence. No wonder Tillerson's mute; he exhausted himself trying to explain all of ExxonMobil's fuckups.

Finally, ethically challenged crony and former Georgia governor Sonny Perdue was appointed secretary of agriculture. It's hard for me to trust a grown man named Sonny, and if I wanted a Perdue in the cabinet, I'd have chosen Frank. At least he can get me a good price on fresh chicken.

C is for Cable TV. Cable television is what Donald Trump watches 24/7 instead of reading. Cable news is Trump's idea of research. It's like watching *Hogan's Heroes* to learn about World War II. It scares the bejeesus out of me to think that national security is now in the hands of Tucker Carlson.

C is for Carnage. In his peppy little inauguration speech, Trump promised to stop the "American carnage." Does he even know what the word *carnage* means? On the very day he gave that speech, unemployment was 4.7 percent, gasoline was $2.29 a gallon, the inflation rate was 2.04 percent, and the stock market was booming. In addition, the crime rate was lower than Sarah Palin's IQ. So, where is all this carnage he's talking about? My guess? It's coming out of Steve Bannon's mouth.

C is for *Casablanca*. The other night, I was watching Turner Classic Movies with my daughter, and one of my favorite movies of all time, *Casablanca*, was on. I said, "Humphrey Bogart was sexy." My daughter was horrified. She said, "Ma, he's short, he lisps, he has buckteeth, and he spits when he talks!" I said, "He was good enough for Lauren Bacall. Who am I to say no?" She said, "Cary Grant was so much better looking." I said, "a lot of good that did me. He was interested in Randolph Scott."

Anyway, the movie ended, and I turned on the news, and right away, there was Donald Trump. Within thirty seconds, I went from Bogey to Bully. And for some weird reason (and by "weird reason," I mean three glasses of pinot noir), I thought, *What if Trump had produced* Casablanca *instead of Warner Bros.?* It would have been a completely different movie. Sam couldn't have played "As Time Goes By," because he would've quit and filed suit for not having been paid in two years; Rick's place would have gone bankrupt; Ingrid Bergman would have been alone at the airport because Trump Airlines had gone broke; and Claude Rains wouldn't have been able to walk into the fog with Bogey because all their LGBTQ rights would have been taken away.

C **is for Casino.** *Casino* is the Sharon Stone movie where she *doesn't* flash her cooch. Casinos are also where Donald Trump made, and lost, millions, and considered fleecing contractors and filing bankruptcies, a.k.a. "business as usual." It's hard for a casino to lose money, but somehow Trump managed to do it. Not personally, of course—he took investors' money and stockholders' money and shifted it from company to company (all the while paying himself a salary), leveraging and relever-aging over and over, paying off his personal debts with corpo-rate funds. He closed three casinos, killed thousands of jobs, and cost investors millions of dollars, all the while lining his own pockets. Turns out Trump's never been "looking out for 'the little guy.'" He's been looking out for the big guy with little hands. What better person to be in charge of U.S. fiscal pol-icy? Alexander Hamilton is rolling over in his grave.

C **is for *Caveat Emptor.*** *Caveat emptor* is Latin for "Let the buyer beware." So, to the people who recently bought Donald Trump the presidency—yes, I'm talking to you, Vladimir and *Fox & Friends*—don't be surprised that it's defective. It's your fault. *Caveat emptor.* You should have seen it coming.

C **is for Charlie Sheen.** For years, Charlie Sheen was the undisputed Most Ridiculous Human Being in America. His diet consisted entirely of drugs, alcohol, cigarettes, and hookers. He spent more time in Betty Ford than Gerald did. But on Inauguration Day Charlie lost that coveted title. That's the day Donald Trump put his hand on a book he'd never read and swore to uphold a document he'd also never read. Forget December 7, 1941. *January 20, 2017,* is the "date which will live in infamy," because on that day, Charlie Sheen was no longer America's Top Hot Mess. The Donald was.

C **is for Choice.** Republicans like to talk about how their health care plan gives Americans the freedom of choice. Yes, you can choose which way you want to die, because, under their plan, you can't *afford* insurance.

Also, Republicans are a little inconsistent on the matter of choice. For example, they don't think women should be able to choose what to do with their own bodies, and they don't think people should be able to choose whom they marry, but they *do* think that churches should be able to choose which politicians they endorse (even though they don't pay taxes), and corporations should be able to choose which politicians they buy. (Maybe politicians should be required to wear the logos of the corporations who've sponsored them, like NASCAR drivers. Pence could wear a Marlboro patch on his sweater, and McConnell could wear an I ♥ THE KOCH BROTHERS on the back of his shell.)

The GOP also gives us really terrible choices in candidates to vote for: Dan Quayle? George W. Bush? Sarah Palin? Donald Trump? For a start, except for *The Pet Goat*, has any of them ever actually cracked a book? I once heard that Sarah Palin was in a library, and a passerby said to her, "What's a nice girl like you doing in a place like this?" and she demurely responded, "A library? I thought this was Home Depot." The Democrats, on the other hand, have come up with Bill Clinton, Al Gore, Joe Biden, Barack Obama, and Hillary Clinton. They may not be everyone's political cup of tea, but none of them is ignorant, stupid, or bat-shit crazy. I don't imagine Donald Trump will be up for reelection in 2020—he'll be sharing a beach house in Vladivostok with you-know-who—so who will the Republicans run? Following their criteria for presidential contenders, I have a few choices for them: Ted Nugent, Gary Busey, Franklin Graham, David Hasselhoff, Paris Hilton, Heidi Montag, Scott Baio, and Brian Griffin, the dog from *Family Guy*. I have no idea if any of them is even a registered voter, but they are all perfect for the next GOP ticket: silly, cartoonish, and free from the burden of facts.

C is for

Chris

Christ

Sorry, I couldn't fit him on one page. Chris Christie, the soon-to-be ex-governor of New Jersey—he has, as of this writing, the lowest approval rating of any governor in the history of governors, the one-man bridge-blocker, the ass-kisser supreme, was named head of the Trump administration's Opioid and Drug Abuse Commission—because who knows better about conquering addictions than a man who orders lunch by the bale? When a waitress asks Christie what he wants from the menu, he says, "Pages two through five." His three-piece suit consists of a jacket, pants, and a crockpot. The local diner offers an "All-Anyone-but-Chris-Christie-Can-Eat" Buffet.

Chris Christie became a national figure (not unlike Yan-

kee Stadium or Mount McKinley) when Hurricane Sandy hit the Eastern Seaboard. Although, it's not clear that all the damage to the Jersey Shore was caused by Sandy—it's entirely possible that Christie jumped into the ocean to go swimming and contributed to the flooding of the one-thousand-mile-long coastline. (For all the science deniers who didn't get that joke, ask your reality-based friends about Archimedes.) When the hurricane hit, Christie did what any governor would do—he ran through the streets of Asbury Park trying to save the pizzerias, hotdog stands, and ice-cream parlors. He also met with President Obama, shook the president's hand, and accepted federal disaster aid, which is what he should have done. (One point for him!) But afterward, Republicans across the country reacted with horror—*horror*, I tell you—that he had not only met with a Democrat, but also thanked him and walked arm in arm with him on a beach. They were appalled; they would much rather have seen New Jersey turned into the Everglades.

So much for the good news about Chris Christie.

As a New Yorker, I got to know Governor Christie long before Hurricane Sandy introduced him to the rest of the country. In a 2011 town hall meeting, a New Jersey woman asked Christie why he was cutting the budget for public schools while sending his own kids to private schools. He graciously answered, "It's none of your business. I don't ask you where you send your kids to school, don't bother me about where I send mine."

Also in 2011, he got into a squabble with state senator Loretta Weinberg over a pension matter. He asked the press, "Can you guys take the bat out on her for once?" At the time, Weinberg was seventy-six. Nice!

At another town hall meeting, when a law student and former Navy SEAL interrupted him, the bloviating bully told the SEAL, "After you graduate from law school, you conduct yourself like that in a courtroom, your rear end is going to be thrown in jail, idiot." What a charmer. Anyone who talks to a Navy SEAL like that is not only rude but stupid.

But the coup de gross, of course, was the infamous Bridgegate scandal. When I first heard that Chris Christie had blocked four lanes of traffic on the George Washington Bridge, I thought, "What the hell did he do, stand in the middle of it?" Eventually, two of the Bridgegate conspirators (and Christie associates) were convicted of crimes and went to jail. But not Christie. He didn't go to jail; he went to Denny's.

For most of 2015 and 2016, Christie served as the world's biggest lapdog, standing behind candidate Trump at every rally and event, smiling and sweating, as though he'd just run the New York City Marathon. (Yeah, right.) Why? Because he knew that Trump rewards loyalty, and he assumed that, if Trump were elected, he'd be a part of the main White House team. He assumed wrong. One of the few things Trump val-

Starting shortstop for the New Jersey Camel Toes

ues more than loyalty is optics, and faster than you can say, "I'd like another pizza, please," Corpulent Chris was gone. He didn't rate high enough on the Teutonic Tyrant's pretty meter and was soon off the team and out of sight. This was a big mistake on The Donald's part. Having Christie in the picture

C is for **Chris Christie**. When a waitress asks Chris Christie what he wants from the menu, he says, "Pages two through five."

standing next to him would only have made him appear slimmer. I personally love to go to the Metropolitan Museum and stand next to Rubens's nudes. Much easier than joining Weight Watchers.

Then, in 2017, like a cyborg returning from the dead, Christie resurfaced when The Donald made him his opioids czar. Chris Christie is now the face of opioids. One thing I know about opioids is that they make you very constipated, which is apt, since Christie is full of shit.

C **is for Chutzpah.** Donald Trump declared April 2017 National Sexual Assault Awareness and Prevention Month. I'm not sure if that meant he intended to bubble-wrap his tiny hands and lock himself in a windowless room until May, or that, for the other eleven months, he's free to grab, fondle, and kiss women against their will. What I *am* sure of is that Donald Trump announcing a "Sexual Assault Prevention Month" is like Bill Cosby announcing a "Week Without Roofies."

C is for Climate Change Deniers. There are two types of Republican leaders who deny climate change: the Craven and the Crazies. The Craven, which is most of them, know full well that climate change is a problem, but they've been bought and paid for by the Koch brothers and the fossil fuel industry, so they have to pretend it doesn't exist. Otherwise, their owners might have to spend a dollar or two fixing it. You know the old rule: "You break it, you buy it."

The other group, the Crazies, is far more worrisome. This is the James Inhofe, Pat Robertson, zealot wing of the party. They seem to believe that climate change, along with every other disaster in the history of the country, including 9/11, is really just God's punishment for homosexuality: You wake up in the morning and instead of finding the newspaper on your front porch, you find the Sea of Japan—and these wackos believe God is doing this because a couple of lesbians in Provincetown exchanged commitment rings.

C is for Cojones. "Chutzpah," for my Hispanic friends.

C is for Comedians. Stephen Colbert caught a lot of flak for a joke he told this year on *The Late Show*. The joke was "The only thing [Trump's] mouth is good for is being Vladimir

Putin's cockholster." Complaints came from all directions: Conservatives were outraged both about the language and that Colbert had said it about Trump, and progressives were upset because they thought it was homophobic. I don't know what other words Stephen could've used to make the joke work: *Penispouch? Sausagesack? Schlongwarmer?* It's not a joke I would tell on TV, but that's not the point. (Anyway, I work in daytime.) The point is: Colbert had the right to tell the joke. And now, with Trump, the world's most thin-skinned person, going after the First Amendment—he wants to change the libel laws to make it easier to sue the media—it's more important than ever to stand up for stand-ups.

You see, it's comedians' *job* to speak truth to power, and to do it in a funny way. Not all comedians, mind you—no one expects Gallagher to stop smashing watermelons and do twenty minutes on the Taft-Hartley Act of 1947—but you get my point. These days, I try. And along with Colbert, my fellow comedians Bill Maher, Samantha Bee, Trevor Noah, John Oliver, and Seth Meyers, are doing the heavy lifting on the left. Dennis Miller serves as a counterpoint on the right. Jon Stewart was the voice of a generation of young voters. And before all of them was the great George Carlin, who said it best: "Governments don't want well-informed, well-educated people capable of critical thinking. That is against their interests. They want obedient workers just smart enough to run the machines and do the paperwork. And just dumb enough to passively accept it." I wish Carlin were still alive; he'd have been having a field day with Trump. And he would probably have had to add *cockholster* to his list of Seven Words You Can Never Say on Television.

C is for Comey. James Comey was the FBI director, a job that is supposed to be politically impartial, yet three days before the presidential election, he announced he was going to review more "possible information" about Hillary Clinton's email server, even though his prior investigation had turned up nothing. Now, in 2017, we find out that at the exact same moment he was making that "impartial" announcement, the FBI was six months into investigating the Trump campaign's ties to Russia and possible election rigging. When asked why he hadn't mentioned *that*, Comey said he wasn't allowed to comment on ongoing investigations (as he did with Hillary). Comey wants us to think he's bipartisan, but he's not bi—I think he was in bed with Trump, though Trump fired him anyway. Now I know what you call someone who says he goes both ways but really goes only one way: a Comeysexual. I hate to say it, but I think Comey may be just as bad as J. Edgar Hoover. As far as I can see, the only difference between James Comey and J. Edgar Hoover is that Hoover wore a junior petite cocktail dress, while Comey is a size 18.

C is for Con Man. There are only two big differences between Charles Ponzi, Bernie Madoff, and Donald Trump. (1) The first two aren't conning people anymore (Ponzi's dead, and

Madoff's in jail), whereas Trump is in his duplicitous prime in the Oval Office; and (2) Ponzi and Madoff both became prison bitches, and thus far Trump has not gone to jail. But if . . . er, I mean *when* Trump gets sent to Leavenworth, my inside sources—yes, I have inside prison sources; I correspond with a couple of lifers I met online; don't judge—tell me that the boys in Cell Block H would love themselves a tangerine-blond Pillsbury Doughboy. He'd be huuuuugely popular, no?

C is for Kellyanne Conway. I've interviewed Kellyanne Conway on *The View* a few times. She seems like a nice person, so I can't imagine what reasons she could have for working for Trump as his minister of propaganda, especially because, before she joined the Trump campaign, she was working on the Ted Cruz campaign. During her time with Cruz, she said a lot of nasty things about Trump. She said he was "vulgar," "unpresidential," and that he had "built his businesses on the backs of the little guy." Then, when Cruz dropped out, she immediately joined Team Trump. I guess every person has her price. (Mine is a shiatsu massage and a pair of Spanx.) What I find interesting, though, is that when she was working for Cruz, she was telling the truth about Trump. Now that she works for Trump, she can't tell the truth at all. The woman lies more than the people ducking for cover during the "Bowling Green Massacre." She made up the term *alternative facts*; she said the crowd at Trump's inauguration was bigger than Obama's; she said that "whatever the president does is presidential"; and on and on and on. But my personal favorite is when she said that our microwaves can be used as surveillance tools.

Has Trump made us so crazy that we believe our appliances are spying on us? Did I just hear my Keurig call me a bitch?

C is for Cuba. I don't want to say Trump is ignorant or ill-informed, but when he was asked what he thought about Cuba, he said, "I loved him in *Jerry Maguire*."

D is for Damage. I remember when George W. Bush became president. I thought, *How much damage could he do in four years*? Surprise! First of all, it wound up being eight years, and we're *still* trying to undo the damage he did—little things, like lying about WMD starting two wars and not paying for them, turning a surplus into a trillion-dollar deficit, causing a housing crisis, and breaking the wall between church and state. At this writing, Trump is on course to make Bush look like Nelson Mandela.

D is for *Dancing with the Stars*. On the heels of the host of *Celebrity Apprentice* becoming the U.S. president, the GOP must be scouring reality TV for its next batch of nominees. Could Bruno Tonioli win the White House in the next election, or will the Republicans have to hunt through past contestants to find someone with the right qualifications to run the country? Maybe Dennis Rodman or Suzanne Somers? How about a Vanilla Ice–Kate Gosselin ticket? Or maybe political heavyweights like Ryan Lochte and Nancy Kerrigan? How about the Countess de Lesseps, since we seem to be returning to a monarchy anyway.

D is for Darwin. I was driving to Costco the other day and I noticed the car to the left of me had a metal fish symbol on the back of its trunk. So, at a red light, I pulled up next to the driver and asked him, "What's up with the fish? Are you a Pisces?" The guy said, "No, I'm a creationist." Before I could say, "Really? So, if God created cars, why did he stick you inside a brown Yugo? Couldn't he come up with a Porsche?" the light changed, and he and Flipper drove off.

In 1859, English naturalist Charles Darwin published *On the Origin of Species*, the benchmark study of the evolution of *Homo sapiens* and other creatures. (FYI: in 2015, an original copy of *On the Origin of Species* sold for approximately $150,000. Today, you can buy a hardcover copy of *The Art of the Deal* for six bucks on Amazon. Just sayin'.) *On the Origin of Species* has been taught to, and understood by, almost everyone on the planet to be the cornerstone of biology, and therefore the basis for modern medicine. Notice I said "almost everyone." That's because a lot of religious Republicans (and religious Democrats, too) don't believe in evolution; they believe in creationism—that is, that God created everything. They cannot fathom that we evolved from apes. No, to creationists, it's much more plausible that an imaginary man in the sky made the whole shebang in about a week.

D is for Dyson Vacuums ... the only things that suck more than the Trump administration.

Without getting into religion—I was born Catholic, and my husband was born Jewish, so we have enough guilt already without me worrying about offending people of faith—I don't know how God could have created everything in seven days. Look, I know how to multitask. I have a job on *The View*, I'm writing a book, I do stand-up, I have a family and a grandchild, I cook, I go out, I do things. Even if God had an amazing personal assistant, I just don't know how He could have done it all in a week. What are the odds He never needed a bathroom break, or had to run to Starbucks for a Venti Latte?

I have a lot of religious friends and family, and I *love* having them over during the Christmas holidays. I decorate the tree, I wrap gifts, I cook turkey and ham, and I revel in the smile on my grandson's face when he opens his presents (and immediately figures out what he could resell them for on eBay). I just don't think faith-based Republicans should be involved with my health care. The question I pose to them is: "If God created everything . . . didn't He also create Charles Darwin?" And what about the appendix, which is about as useless as Jeff Sessions at an NAACP meeting?

D is for Deal. One of TV's longest-running game shows is *Let's Make a Deal*. It began in 1963, starring Monty Hall and the lovely Carol Merrill, whose job was to smile and point to boxes, doors, and prizes. Contestants were given a prize, and then they had to decide whether to keep that prize or to trade it in for an unknown item hidden in a box or behind a door. The fun was not knowing which deal to take. On the show, everyone, including Monty Hall, was hoping each contestant would make the right deal and walk away happy.

Thank God Donald Trump didn't host that game show. No one would have walked away happy. That's because the way you or I would define a "good deal," is not the way Donald Trump defines it. I was taught that a good deal is one in which all sides do well and walk away satisfied. Thus, the phrase "Everybody wins." Trump's idea of a good deal is when *he* does well and walks away happy, and to hell with everyone else. *Let's Make a Deal* is still on the air, with Wayne Brady as the host. Maybe Wayne can convince Trump to come on the show as a contestant.

Contestant Trump is given a fifty-thousand-dollar Rolex watch. But that's not good enough, so he decides to trade it in for what's behind door Number One. And behind door Number One is . . . voilà! A two-week stay in Cuba with Rosie O'Donnell and Hillary Clinton, who are conducting a seminar on the history of the women's movement. Guest lecturers include Elizabeth Warren, Meryl Streep, Rosie Perez, and the entire cast of Glee. I can only dream . . .

D is for Dear Abby. "Dear Abby" was the most famous advice column of all time. In fact, "Abigail Van Buren" (the pen name of the column's creator, Pauline Phillips) was so good that even though she's now dead, people are still writing to her. And she still answers! A recent letter has been discovered and leaked to me, and as a public service, I'm leaking it to you:

Dear Abby,

My husband, Lenny, and I live at 1601 Pennsylvania Avenue, Washington, DC. We have new neighbors, and they—mostly he—are horrible. The people who moved out were lovely. I think the husband did something in government, and the wife was always gardening and working out. They were very smart (I hear he went to

Harvard!) and had two teenage daughters and a couple of
dogs. Beyond nice!

Long story short, they moved out on January 19, and the
next day, this loud, obnoxious orange guy moved in with a
gorgeous European woman. I don't know if she's the nanny
or the housekeeper, because she was here for only a day,
and I haven't seen her since. Might've been a "date."

Then, a pretty blond girl moved in. She kept calling
him "Daddy."

Since then, a parade of creepy people keeps coming
and going. This one oily guy, Steve Something-or-other,
comes by every single day, and within minutes, it's
complete chaos, with FBI and the NSA and CIA teams all
over the neighborhood.

Lenny and I don't know what to do. We love our house,
but we can't live like this. Should we sell? Should we move?
We've tried to get the new neighbor on the phone, but his
"daughter" keeps telling us he can't talk because their
wires were tapped. We're desperate. What should we do?

Ruth, Washington, DC

Dear Ruth,

You and Lenny should be patient. Stay calm and stay
put. I have a feeling these new neighbors won't be living
there for very long.
Good luck!

Abby

D **is for Delusion**. According to Dictionary.com, *delusion* is defined as "a false belief held despite strong evidence against it." For example, Donald Trump's saying that there were three million illegal votes cast for Hillary Clinton? A delusion. Or that President Obama wiretapped Trump Tower? Delusion. Or that thousands of Muslims in New Jersey were cheering when the towers fell on 9/11? Delusion. Or that Trump's inaugural crowd was larger than Obama's? You guessed it.

Being delusional is classified as a form of mental illness. When I said on TV that Trump is mentally ill, Bill O'Reilly called me disrespectful. Now, if anybody knows how to be respectful, it's Bill O'Reilly. Is it respectful to say that all Muslims are terrorists, like he did on *The View* the day Whoopi Goldberg and I walked off our own show? Is it respectful to say that Maxine Waters's hair looks like a James Brown wig? And is it respectful as Trump himself said to "grab them by the pussy"? In the words of the great Aretha Franklin, R-E-S-P-E-C-T. Find out what it means to me.

D **is for Dementia**. Donald Trump says so many outrageous things, and contradicts himself so often, I'm beginning to worry he might have some sort of dementia. He says one thing at 2:00, something else at 3:00, a completely different thing at 4:00, and at 6:00 he denies having said anything at all.

"I met Putin once, a long time ago. We got along great."

"I've never met Putin."

"Putin and I have a very good relationship."

"I don't think I've ever spoken to Putin."

"If I've met him, I don't remember."

How could he not remember meeting Vladimir Putin? If Trump were asked, "Do you remember meeting Sol Fishman, the president of the Boca Raton B'nai B'rith?" and he couldn't remember? Fine. I'd understand. But Vladimir Putin? There's *one* Russian dictator in the entire world, and it's him, and Trump can't remember if they met? When Donald went to staff his White House, he somehow remembered Omarosa, and she was nothing more than a contestant on *The Apprentice*, and she's not even one-third as bad as Putin. (Although she was a pain in the ass the last time she was on *The View*.)

If Donald Trump *does* have dementia and can't remember what he's saying, then, for both his sake and ours, we should get him some help. If he doesn't have dementia, and he's just lying all the time, fuck him.

P.S. Twice, I think I heard him call Melania, "Mr. Watkins." Just sayin'.

D is for Denial. This is the state where most of my Blue state friends are moving to. It's cheaper than moving to Canada or Europe. It's also the state where many Trump supporters live; it's located right between Xanadu and Fantasyland.

D is for Betsy DeVos. I'm a feminist and I want women to do well—just not *this* woman. (FYI: when I say I'm a feminist, I mean I believe in equal pay, equal opportunity, paid maternity leave, etc. It also means that I've had lunch with Gloria Steinem and gone hat shopping with Bella Abzug.) Betsy DeVos is, in my opinion, the Antichrist of education. If I went through the entire U.S. phone book, it would be hard to find anyone less qualified or more wildly inappropriate for this position. The Department of Education is all about *public* schools. Betsy DeVos is all about private schools, charter schools, Christian schools, and school voucher programs. She cares less about public schools than I care about mixed martial arts. (Truth be told, I don't even know what they are. One night, my husband was channel-surfing and he stopped on a channel with two men kicking the shit out of each other. He told me it was a mixed martial arts fight. I thought it was *The Jerry Springer Show*. I still don't understand how kicking, punching, and biting are considered "arts." Does this mean ballet, opera, and decoupage are now considered "sports"?) Putting Betsy DeVos in charge of public education is like putting gravel in your lubricant: it's counterproductive and could cause permanent long-term damage.

D is for Diet. Believe it or not, Donald Trump's presidency may be very good for women's empowerment and self-esteem. Think about it: Trump admits he judges women on their appearance and weight, and ogles only women who are supermodels or skinny bitches. So, unless you want to be ogled (or, worse yet, groped) by Donald J. Trump, it's time to start packin' on the pounds. Fuck Jenny Craig. Screw Nutri-System. Get me Ben and Jerry on the line! Hurry up. I need me some Chunky Monkey!

D **is for Disaster.** *Disaster* is one of Donald Trump's favorite words, along with *me*, *I*, *I'm*, *my*, and *mine*. According to Trump, *everything* is a disaster. In March 2016, way before he was semi-elected president, the *Chicago Tribune* listed fifty things Donald J. Trump has called (mostly in tweets) "disasters." Here is a *partial* list:

- The U.S. economy
- The U.S. border
- The U.S. military
- The U.S. deal with Iran
- Mitt Romney as a presidential candidate
- Obama's executive orders
- Former New York City mayor Ed Koch
- The Electoral College
- George W. Bush
- Ken Starr
- Obamacare
- Supreme Court justice John Roberts
- The North American Free Trade Agreement
- Hillary Clinton in general

Clearly, there are other, more accurate, words to describe most of these. For example, Leona Helmsley was a greedy bitch; Ken Starr is a sleazy right-wing tool; Ed Koch was a whiny mama's boy with male-pattern baldness and child-bearing hips; George W. Bush was a bumbling simpleton who needed the Heimlich Maneuver three times a week; and Mitt Romney is a zillionaire Mormon whose sideburns wear magic underpants.

Since very few things are true disasters, Donald Trump's overuse of the word is troubling, because (1) it minimizes and diminishes the pain caused by real disasters, and (2) it exaggerates the gravity of things that are not disasters.

Here's a short list of things that really have been or are disasters:

- The *Titanic* sinking
- Pearl Harbor
- 9/11
- The AIDS crisis
- Famine
- Earthquakes
- Tsunamis
- Hurricanes
- *Godfather III*

D is for **Drinking.** There's an old adage that when people get drunk, they lose their inhibitions and say what they really mean. I'm betting this is why Trump doesn't drink. I know this adage is true because I always had a glass or two or six of white wine before I sat down to work on this book. Pence doesn't drink, either, apparently worried he might find himself in a Bloomingdale's window wearing a teddy and six-inch heels and singing "I Will Survive."

Run, they told him, Pa-Drumpf-Drumpf-Drumpf-Drumpf

A new dic-ta-tor's born, Pa-Drumpf-Drumpf-Drumpf-Drumpf

D is for **Drumpf.** By now, everyone knows that Donald Trump's original family name is "Drumpf," and that his grandfather, Friedrich Drumpf, changed it to "Trump" when he came to America from Germany. You read that correctly: Donald Trump's grandfather was an immigrant.

I don't blame Friedrich for changing the family name from "Drumpf" to "Trump." "Drumpf" is a pretty clunky name, although it could have been worse; it could have been "Dump." Then we'd have Donald Dump. And his driver's license would read, "Dump, Donald." Take away the comma, and that's a movement I can get behind.

It's not uncommon for notable people to change their family names: Cary Grant's real name was Archibald Leach, Judy Garland's real name was Frances Gumm, Tony Curtis was Bernie Schwartz, and Rock Hudson was Doris Nussbaum.

D is for **Dyson** Vacuums. The only things that suck more than the Trump administration.

D is for **Dystopia.** During the campaign (and in the early stages of the administration), Team Trump, led by Field Marshal Bannon, painted America as crumbling and collapsing. Liberals know that that's not true, that we are not living in a dystopia. Trump's base believes dystopia is either a country in Europe or a blood pressure medicine. What *is* crumbling is Trump's agenda. And what will be happening soon is they'll all be moving to Dystopia and wearing leftover outfits from *Fiddler on the Roof.*

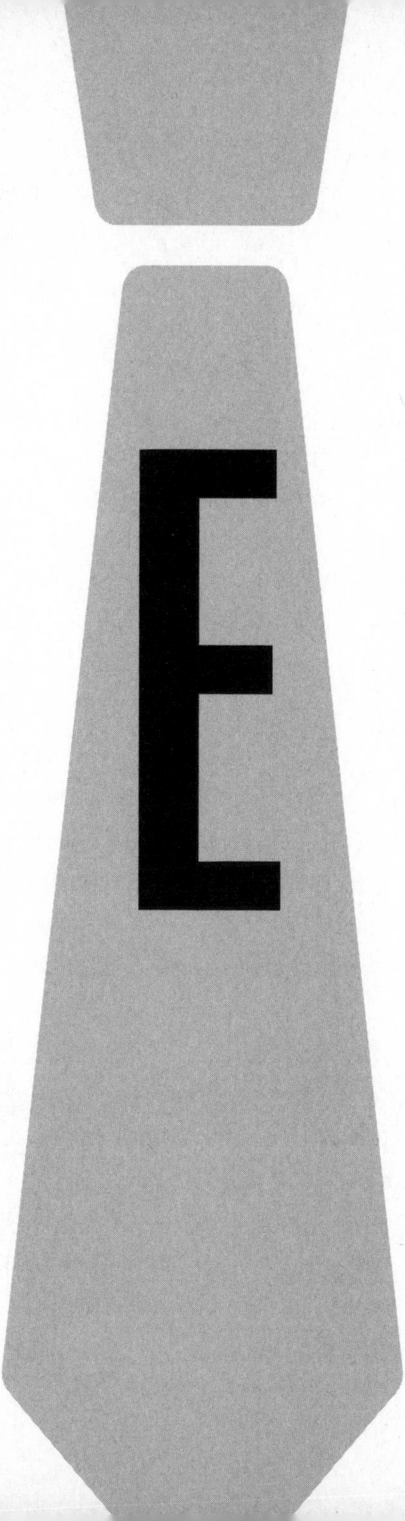
E

E is for Economy. Trump rants and raves that he inherited an economic mess from Obama, but, shockingly, that's not true. Other than "sixty-nine" and the figures making up a winning lottery ticket, numbers are boring, but here are a few worth remembering: According to FactCheck.org, when President Obama took office, the economy had lost 4.4 million jobs in the previous twelve months. When Trump took office, the economy had *added* 2.2 million jobs over the previous twelve months, and had *gained* jobs for *seventy-five* consecutive months, a record. When Obama took office, unemployment was 7.8 percent; when Trump took office, it was 4.7 percent. And corporate growth was running at near-record levels during the Obama years. There are negatives, to be sure, such as a slow growth rate and stagnating wages, but overall, Obama left Trump a much better hand than the one W. left Obama. The one negative I'm having the most trouble with is that when Obama took office, a Starbucks Venti Cappuccino cost $3.75. Now, it's $287,000. What's up with that? (Just kidding, Howard Schultz—you are one of the good guys.)

E is for Education. During the 2016 campaign, Donald Trump said, "I love the poorly educated." Of course he does! They're easier to dupe, and he can fool them into helping him get what he wants (which is more money for him, basically). If Trump loves the poorly educated so much, how come he didn't appoint any of them to his Cabinet? (As noted in the Cs, his Cabinet may be filled with terrible, awful, and possibly mendacious people, but at least they all went to college.) When he appoints CEOs and executives to head up the gazillion companies he claims to own, do you think he hires any eighth-grade dropouts to run them?

Every civilized country in the world that calls itself a democracy has free higher education. Not us. That's because, every chance they get, Republicans cut the education budget, making it harder for kids to go to college and way harder to pay for it. Why? Because they *don't want their voters to go to college*. You see, the less info voters have, the less likely they are to ask questions. Questions like: "How come our tax dollars pay for your health insurance but not ours?" or, "Do you really want my nana to eat cat food?" or "Does Congressman Louie Gohmert have to wear a helmet just to eat soup?"

The mind is a muscle—use it or lose it. I may not do sit-ups or bench presses, but I exercise my brain as often as I can. I don't mean I lay my head on the treadmill for twenty minutes—my hair would look terrible—but every morning, I read the papers, watch the news, do crossword puzzles, and write letters and emails to people who post annoying cat videos.

E is for Eeeeewww!

Yeah, she's really something, and what a beauty, that one. If I weren't happily married and, ya' know, her father . . .

—Donald Trump, speaking about his daughter Ivanka on *The Howard Stern Show*, 2004

EEEEEWWW IS RIGHT!

E is for Eisenhower. Dwight D. Eisenhower was the last Republican president I liked. He was quiet, he didn't bother anybody, he was the commander of the Allied Expeditionary Forces on D-Day, and he let Mamie comb out her bangs in the sink. He also famously warned us to be very wary of the military-industrial complex. We didn't listen. Shame on us.

E is for Elephant. Elephants are giant, lumbering creatures that poop all over everything, so it's fitting that the elephant is the symbol for the Republican Party. But it wasn't the party's first choice. Before they settled on the meandering pachyderm they went through other options for creatures that would fairly represent them:

- **SLUG:** a disgusting thing that serves no purpose and can be killed with salt.
- **CATFISH:** a slithery bottom-feeder.
- **MOUNTAIN LION:** a vicious killer that preys on the small and weak.
- **LAUGHING HYENA:** a mammal that thinks it's hysterical when the anteater gets its tongue stuck in a log.
- **KOALA:** a marsupial that sits around all day doing nothing.
- **PRAYING MANTIS:** an insect that went to court to change its name to "praying mantis" because it was forced to by creationist caterpillars.

- **FLY:** an insect that spends most of its time dancing in pieces of poop or buzzing around public restrooms.

E is for Eloquence. Words matter, and contrary to what Donald Trump said in December 2015—"I know words. I have the best words"—he doesn't. He seems to know about twenty-five or thirty words, which he repeats over and over, and not always in the right order. I think my dogs have a more extensive vocabulary. In fact, according to Dr. Stanley Coren, an expert in canine communication, the average dog can understand 165 words. Border collies, which are the smartest dogs, can learn up to a thousand words. Not only that, dogs can learn in any language they're taught. Which makes me think, spare me Trump's ridiculous border wall. Just put a couple of bilingual collies on the border and let them handle illegal immigration. They won't bite, they won't rip families apart, and they won't cost twenty billion dollars. A couple of chew toys and a case of Alpo, and they're good to go.

I miss President Obama's soaring oratory. Everyone says his speeches were the kind of speeches you hear in gospel churches. I haven't spent much time in gospel churches—I was raised to listen to priests telling me not to go to Queens College because there were "Commies there."

Presidents *should* be able to give good speeches; they're supposed to be statesmen. Democrats understand that. Franklin Roosevelt said, "The only thing we have to fear is fear itself." JFK said, "Ask not what your country can do for you, ask what you can do for your country." Bill Clinton said,

"Monica, don't bang your head on the drawer." What do we get from Donald Trump? "I have big words." The last Republican who came even marginally close to speaking eloquently was George Bush Sr., and I don't exactly consider "Read my lips, no new taxes" scintillating oratory, but at least it was a full sentence. "I see a thousand points of light!" A lovely sentiment, but I had no idea what he was talking about. I thought maybe he was seeing floaters.

Republicans call Ronald Reagan "the great communicator," and compare him to Kennedy. They always cite the speech when Reagan said, "Mr. Gorbachev, tear down this wall," as though it's great oratory. It sounds like Reagan was having a Shirley Temple–like tantrum, whimpering, holding his breath, and stamping his feet: "Tear down this wall. Me mad!"

E is for Empathy. This is the one gene that Trump and his congressional Republicans seem to be missing. I think they used to have it, but somehow, over time, it mutated, evolving into a mean gene, which is ironic, since a lot of them don't even believe in evolution.

E is for English. Donald Trump says that everyone in America should learn to speak English. Ironic, coming from a seventy-year-old man who speaks English at a sixth-grade level. He says it will help assimilation, and while that's a fair topic for discussion, our foreign-born residents aren't going to wake up one morning and magically start speaking English. They'll need to be taught. And while linguistics experts say it's more difficult for adults to learn new languages than children, it can be done. Melania Trump is said to speak five languages. She can say, "I want a divorce," in English, French, German, Serbian, and Slovene. And don't forget, President Obama learned to speak English while he was growing up in Kenya.

E is for Estrogen. Something the White House is in desperate need of. There's so much testosterone in the West Wing, it's like a gay bar, except without the good-looking men. Trump had a press conference touting all the women in his administration. There were four or five, depending on whether Steve Bannon is transitioning.

E is for Eugenics. Can you guess when and where eugenics became a popular practice? If you said "the 1930s" and "Germany," you win the grand prize. Do you know when and where eugenics became *un*popular? If you said "1945" and "everywhere," you win again! (And again, there's no prize.) Do you know who seems to be a fan of eugenics in 2017? If you said "Donald Trump," you're on a roll. Here are some actual quotes from our Teuton in chief:

E is for Evangelicals. Where in the Bible does it say, "Thou shalt grab thy neighbor by the pussy"? Is it Leviticus or Genesis?

- "All men are created equal. Well, it's not true. 'Cause some are smart, some aren't."

- "Do we believe in the gene thing? I mean, I do."
- "I have great genes and all that stuff, which I'm a believer in."

If Trump has such great and powerful genes, how come none of his kids looks like him? Ivanka and Hans and Fritz look like Ivana; Barron looks like Melania; and Tiffany? We rarely see her, so I'm stumped on that one. And by the way, how come none of them has an orange face or salmon-colored hair? Answer me that!

E **is for Europe.** Once, the majority of the countries in Europe were our allies, but ever since Trump took over, they're running away faster than Katy Perry at a Taylor Swift concert. Yet, Donald Trump doesn't seem to be worried by these defections. I'm not sure if it's because he doesn't know about them, or because he figures Europe will be part of Russia by the end of his first term anyway.

Think about it this way: Trump is not welcome in Europe, a continent that's more than happy to have Roman Polanski wandering the streets. I'm not sure if it's because Europeans hate his politics or his personality. He's ill-mannered, for sure—when Angela Merkel came to the White House, Trump wouldn't shake her hand. Lucky her: you never know where those little paws have been.

But he hasn't stopped at Europe. He's spreading his rudeness all over the world. You want to talk amazing? Trump has alienated Australia, of all places. How crude and nasty do you have to be to get the Australians mad at you? These people invite you to their houses the minute they meet you. (Of course, you never go: it's a bloody twenty-four-hour flight.) Mel Gibson notwithstanding, the Aussies are fabulous! All they do is drink and laugh and eat peanut butter-and-dingo sandwiches; they're beyond nice—and *they* can't stand him. I'll bet if Donald Trump goes to the North Pole, within three weeks, the Eskimos will be telling him to "Go fuck himself" in Inuit.

E **is for Evangelicals.** Evangelicals are Protestant Christians who have been "born again," read the Bible as literal fact, have "turned away from sin, and are devoted to spreading the Word." Born again? The first time was bad enough.

Yet, in the 2016 election, when they had a choice to support a religious woman who is a mother and grandmother, has been married to the same man for forty-one years, and has devoted her entire adult life to public service and helping children, *or* an ignorant, amoral, lying, vulgar adulterer with five children by three different wives . . . they went with the adulterer. They chose a man who alleges that he grabs women by their privates without asking, who makes fun of the handicapped, who disses war heroes, who calls women derogatory names, and who hasn't seen the inside of a church since Ivanka was a virgin. So, I ask these evangelicals, where in the Bible does it say, "Thou shalt grab thy neighbor by the pussy"? Is it Leviticus or Genesis?

Donald J. Trump   Follow

@realDonaldTrump

Any negative polls are fake news, just like the CNN,
ABC, NBC polls in the election. Sorry, people want
border security and extreme vetting.

Donald J. Trump   Follow

@realDonaldTrump

FAKE NEWS—A TOTAL POLITICAL WITCH HUNT!

Donald J. Trump   Follow

@realDonaldTrump

Totally made up facts by sleazebag political operatives,
both Democrats and Republicans—FAKE NEWS!
Russia says nothing exists.

is for Fake News. There's no such thing as "fake news"—
unless, of course, you count Fox as news, in which case, I
stand corrected. *Fake news* is the term Donald Trump invented
to describe any factual stories or journalistic reporting that is
unfavorable to him or hurts his feelings.

Last night, I had dinner at an Italian restaurant and I
ordered the Clams Casino (which, by the way, is the name I
would use if I were a stripper). The clams weren't very good—
they were overcooked and chewy—but I didn't jump up and
start yelling at the chef that they were fake clams or it was fake
food. I just didn't finish them. The end. When Trump started

going out with Marla Maples, she was quoted in a headline in the *New York Post* that read, "Best Sex I Ever Had!" Now *that's* what I call fake news.

F is for Falsehood. *Falsehood* is the word the media and cowardly members of Congress use instead of *lie* when talking about Donald Trump's penchant for saying things that aren't true. It's kind of like calling an hour with a hooker a "date."

F is for Fiddle. Emperor Nero is said to have fiddled while Rome burned. The only differences between Nero and Emperor Trump are (1) Trump doesn't play a musical instrument, and Nero did; (2) Trump doesn't live in Italy; Nero did; and (3) Trump started the fire; Nero didn't. I mean this both literally (Trump denies climate change) and metaphorically (he's torching democracy). By the way, every time I see him on TV, my eyes start to burn. He's a visual arsonist.

F is for Filibuster. One of my favorite movies is *Mr. Smith Goes to Washington*, in which Jimmy Stewart filibusters for hours on the Senate floor until he collapses. In the old days, a senator who was filibustering actually had to stand up and speak for as long as he could. Nowadays, they only have to *declare* a filibuster, and they can sit there doing crossword puzzles or listening to Pat Boone on their Walkmans while thinking of new ways to wreck the Constitution. I think if they want to filibuster like Jimmy Stewart, then they should have to stand there and talk like Jimmy Stewart. I realize that listening to Ted Cruz speak is worse than listening to a chorus of men coughing up phlegm in a stuck elevator, but look on the bright side—eventually Ted would collapse.

is for Florida. If Trump and Congress cut Social Security and Medicare, Florida is going to be really pissed off. Florida has lots of old people. The average age of a person living in Florida is "dead." Cut their benefits, and you can bet that angry seniors will take to the streets—they'll be yelling and chanting and coughing. They'll start the Million Nana March. Okay, it might not be a march. It might be more of a shuffle but they'll protest—and there's nothing scarier than a bunch of senior citizens on Viagra driving their motorized wheelchairs toward you. If they really get mad, their dentures could be used as weapons.

is for Flynn. Michael Flynn was Trump's first national security advisor. Turns out it was a temp job. Flynn is an old Irish name, meaning "Haldeman and Erlichman."

is for Foreign Relations Committee. This is what Donald Trump uses to meet his wives.

is for Foreplay. Note to Trump voters, the Trump agenda is like foreplay: promises of free health care, jobs, jobs, jobs, and low taxes . . . It's teasing and teasing and teasing, but eventually you know you're going to get screwed.

F is for Fracking. Fracking, the process of injecting liquid into subterranean rock at high pressure to force out oil or gas, is one of the resource extraction methods our *real* presidents, the Koch brothers, are in favor of—not because it's good for the country, but because it's good for *them*. They have lots of money invested in fracking. And after buying Congress, they'd like some return on their investment. If fracking were safe and regulated, it might be a good stop-gap measure until we transferred our energy sources from fossil fuel to wind and solar. But right now, fracking is tied to water contamination and . . . earthquakes. Yes, you read that right. Oklahoma is known as the Sooner State, but since they began fracking there, you'd sooner get caught in an earthquake than a tornado. According to *60 Minutes*, in 2015 there were 907 earthquakes in Oklahoma. Nine hundred seven! Tulsa shakes more than the ground under Chris Christie's feet.

F is for Foreign Relations Committee. This is what Donald Trump uses to meet his wives.

F is for Fraud. Donald "I Never Settle Lawsuits" Trump recently settled a $25 million lawsuit for fraud against Trump University. Twenty-five million dollars. That's a lot of diplomas. Apparently, Trump University wasn't actually a university, and a number of students sued for fraud. (How the students didn't know it was a scam is beyond me. The courses included Snake Oil 101, The Basics of Bilking, and Fleecing for Dummies. Not only that, but Bernie Madoff was a professor emeritus.) Anyway, Trump had to pay out $25 mill, and the "university" is no more. Trump U? FU is more like it.

Trump University Course Offerings

Making Your Mark
How to pick a sucker in less than fifteen minutes. The tell-tale signs that a person is a patsy. Ten easy steps to turn a dope into a dupe.

Stakes and Steaks
From rustling cattle to bankrupting the butcher, this class teaches all you need to know about opening, and closing, a beef business—in a bull market!

Fly Me to the Ground

Starting an airline is easy. Running one into the ground takes talent. This "crash" course teaches you how to turn a loss leader into a massive tax write-off.

Advanced Pandering

How to make everyone you deal with think they're happy? Learn how to tell 'em what they want to hear. Turn brown-nosing into a shit-eatin' grin.

Tweet Your Way to the Top

Build your brand by saying outrageous and crazy things in fewer than 140 characters. A must-take class for students with limited vocabularies.

You Are Your Greater Good

Find out why altruism, charity, and ethics are bad for business, and learn how to make selfishness an asset.

The Art of the Feel

This course offers the ins and outs of pussy-grabbing. Find out how even you, a nonfamous commoner, can sexually assault women and brag about it later.

How to Make John Maynard Keynes Your Bitch

The British economist's theories spawned the rise of modern liberalism in the West. Sad! Keynes bad; Milton Friedman (economic adviser to Reagan and Thatcher) good. Guest speakers include the four people who did well in the United States as a result of Reaganomics. The dean of Trump University, Donald Trump, will make a (paid) appearance.

Ten Cents on the Dollar
Why pay 100 percent of what you owe employees, contractors, or business partners when there are semilegal ways to pay ten cents on the dollar?

Preparing a Prenup
Find out how to protect your investment. Learn how to buy silence at a fraction of the market rate. Get helpful tips on how to "convince" your exes to say nice things about you.

Just Say No
Learn how to put the old adage "Rules are for losers" into practice. This course will teach you how to hide assets, open shell companies, and bury funds overseas. As a bonus, it offers free lessons in conversational Russian.

F **is for Freedom.** Republicans are obsessed with the word *freedom*: individual freedom, personal freedom, financial freedom, religious freedom—they can't get enough. They yell it all the time, "Freedom! Freedom! Freedom!" It's like they have Tourette's syndrome. They could be at a funeral and they'd jump up on top of the deceased and start yelling, "Freedom! Freedom! Freedom!" trying to round up a few more votes.

F is for Freedom Caucus. The Freedom Caucus is a group of very conservative House Republicans who get together to vote against anything that might extend freedoms to American people they don't happen to like. For example, freedom to get a doctor to remove your brain tumor without sending your entire family to a homeless shelter, or freedom to repair bridges and tunnels that are about to collapse. The members of the Freedom Caucus want the freedom to know who's peeing in the stall next to them, and if they don't approve of that person, she'll have to hold it in. They want the freedom to carry guns everywhere, and they want insurance companies to have the freedom to deny coverage because a bullet hole is a preexisting condition.

They shut down the Republican health care plan because it gave too *much* help to poor people and the elderly. Who's in the Freedom Caucus? There are about three dozen members—too many to list here, but three prominent names are the congressmen Andy Biggs, Dave Brat, and Ted Yoho. That's right, Biggs, Brat, and Yoho. Sounds like a law firm in Toyland.

F is for Freedom Fries. The dumbest thing I've ever heard in my entire life, and I've heard a lot of dumb things. Don't forget: I was a teacher. If you say, "Billy, what's the capital of the United States?" and he replies, "Cantaloupe," he's not going to be in Mensa, he's going to be in Congress. Which brings me to former Republican congressman Bob Ney, of Ohio. In 2003, when France decided not to support the U.S. invasion of Iraq, Ney decided that its betrayal of America was so awful and so egregious that he had to take the strongest action he could possibly take. Enraged, he grabbed his Magic Marker, ran downstairs to the basement of the Capitol Building, and stormed the cafeteria. And with one violent flourish of his Sharpie, he changed the name of French fries to "Freedom fries"! *Sacre bleu!* That'll show them.

This histrionic display reminds me of Donald Trump. Is it possible that Bob Ney is Trump's role model? Since Trump is pissed at Canada, England, and Mexico, how long will it be before we have to refer to Canadian bacon as "Constitutional bacon," English breakfast tea as "Old Glory breakfast tea," and Mexican jumping beans as "jingoistic jumping beans." I can't wait for that executive order signing ceremony.

G is for **Gall Bladder.** The gall bladder is like Vice President Mike Pence. It serves no major purpose other than to store bile, and we can live happily without it.

G is for **GITMO.** The U.S. federal prison located in Guantánamo Bay, Cuba. After 9/11, President Bush and his vice president, Lon Chaney, began imprisoning, warehousing, and torturing people suspected of being terrorists. *Suspected*, not convicted, and, in many cases, not even charged or tried. President Obama tried closing GITMO down, and failed, but Trump plans on keeping it open and filling it up, again. Is this because he thinks he's keeping America safe, or because he plans on making it the site of the next great new Trump Hotel and Casino? I can see it now: gold-plated cell doors, marble torture chambers, shiny brass leg irons, and electric chairs with gilt head attachments. Every time you pull the handle on a slot machine, it electrocutes a detainee from the Middle East. Kill one, get one free!

G is for **Guns.** If guns don't kill people, why do we give our soldiers guns rather than spatulas?

G is for **Giuliani.** At some point during the 2016 campaign, "America's mayor," Rudy Giuliani, turned into "America's maniac." He began ranting and raving and foaming at the mouth. I didn't know whether to call 9–1–1 or Cesar Millan.

G is for *Glee*. The TV show *Glee*, which ran on Fox for six years, from 2009 to 2015, was a send-up of teenage life in the Midwest. It tried to entertain, but also to send a message: the characters were diverse, multicultural, and of different sexual orientations. The show was a hit, but very annoying. No matter what the story line was, no matter how intense the drama, in the middle of a scene, someone would burst into song. Who needs that? Who does that? If I'm at Macy's buying a brassiere, do I need the sales clerk to burst into a rousing rendition of "Climb Ev'ry Mountain"? No. I think if *Glee* had had fewer impromptu show tunes and more acting, it might still be on the air. That said, on the day that Donald Trump gets impeached, I plan to run out into the street and burst into "Happy Days Are Here Again."

G is for God. Republican politicians *love* God. Not like or care for, but *love*. They love Him almost as much as they love loitering in men's rooms. They try to put God into every political discussion. "Well, it's God's will that ExxonMobil got a twenty-million-dollar tax break," or, "It's God's will that Betsy DeVos's brother's company, Blackwater Security, got a billion-dollar no-bid contract." So, it makes perfect sense that Donald Trump won the Republican nomination for president. He thinks he *is* God.

G is for Gold. Donald Trump loves gold. Ever been to one of his hotels? It's shocking. The glare is so bright it can cause hysterical blindness. (Not unlike when he speaks, which can cause hysterical deafness.) Or to his New York City apartment? Everything is gold: the ceiling, the fixtures, the walls, the people. It's like living in Flava Flav's mouth.

They say money can't buy happiness.Apparently, it can't buy taste, either.

G is for Gold(en Shower). There have been rumors of a secret dossier that reveals that the Russians have a sex tape of Donald Trump and some prostitutes engaging in . . . well, how do I put this nicely? The Donald witnessing the ladies "christening" a bed the Obamas once slept in.

I don't know if it's true, and I personally don't care what Trump does in the bedroom (or bathroom); it's none of my business. If he enjoys using Svetlana as a showerhead, who am I to judge? There are plenty of fetishes that are *a lot* weirder than that:

Actirasty: Becoming aroused by the sun's rays. Not worried too much about this one; Trump's already orange. (FYI: Icarus wasn't an adventurer; he was just horny.)

Agalmatophilia: Becoming aroused by statues. Better keep Donald away from the Lincoln Memorial—and from Martha Stewart.

Climacophilia: Becoming aroused by falling downstairs. Now we know why Betty Ford stayed with Gerry all those years.

Gerontophilia: Being aroused by old people. I didn't know this was a fetish. I just think Larry King is really hot. *Grrrr . . .*

Nebulophilia: Being aroused by fog. That would explain Prince Charles's attraction to Camilla.

Given all Trump's alleged ties to Russia, his getting Siberian hookers to pish on command is the least of my concerns.

G is for Golf. On at least twenty-six occasions, Donald Trump tweeted petty complaints and nasty comments about President Obama playing (too much) golf. Yet, as president, Trump himself has spent pretty much every weekend on a golf course.

Forget the hypocrisy, why was Trump so annoyed that Obama played golf? Is it because Obama is a better golfer? Or maybe it's that Obama isn't playing on *Trump's* courses? Or . . .

G is for Government. Ronald Reagan used to say, "Government is the problem." The way *he* ran it, yes; the way Bill Clinton and Obama ran it, no. It's hard for me to take anything Reagan said seriously. The man called his wife "Mommy." That is not a sign of astute wisdom or critical thinking; it's a sign of Oedipal issues and bed-wetting. In an effort to save money on school lunches, Reagan considered ketchup a vegetable. Even worse, he privately said that he considered Kleenex a dessert and spackle a salad dressing. And this, ladies and gentlemen, is the man Republicans hold up as the beacon of leadership. Oh wait, I forgot to mention government cheese.

G is for **Government Cheese.** In 1981, Reagan decided to help poor people—not by giving them jobs or education or opportunities, but by giving them cheese. As part of the recently passed Farm Bill, he decided to give poor people government-surplus cheese. Because nothing says "I care" like a block of Limburger. And not for nothing, cheese is binding. Those poor people were not only down on their luck and struggling, but now they were constipated, too. This may be why people say that the Republicans don't give a shit.

G is for **Grandma and Grandpa.** Who doesn't love Nana and Pop? Trump and his friends, that's who, since they are not counted as close relatives in his travel ban if they come from the wrong countries. They don't seem to care much about the grandparents who were born here either. In every budget proposal they put forth, they try to cut Medicare and privatize Social Security. This is not going to work. When animals in the wild get old and sick, they go off into the woods to die. Old people don't do that. They go off to Florida and play cards and undertip the waitstaff. As for privatizing, that means letting private businessmen take care of your grandparents— businessmen like Donald Trump. If that's the plan, we all might as well just give up the card games and go wandering into the woods with the other animals.

Rudy became "America's mayor" after 9/11—a nickname he milked like a dairy cow in heat. To this day, Giuliani references 9/11 every couple of minutes. If you ask him what time it is, he'll say, "Sixteen years, eighty-three days, four hours, and twenty-six minutes since nine-eleven." In bed, his safe word is *Osama*; he refers to his penis as "the Freedom Tower." Must I go on?

Listen, on September 11, 2001, Giuliani did what any mayor of a city under attack would have done—nothing more, nothing less. Do Giuliani supporters think that if David Dinkins had still been mayor on that day he would've played tennis at the Asphalt Green instead?

If all this isn't enough to explain why Trump liked Rudy, here's the coup de grace-less: women. Like Trump, Giuliani has been married three times. Like Trump, he cheated on wife number two with wife number three; and like Trump, he takes special delight in humiliating his ex-wives. This proves that, as my friend Mitch once said, "Women will go for anything."

G is for Guns. Republicans love guns more than Rush Limbaugh loves pie. They're obsessed with them (especially the pro-lifers; ironic, no?). I ran into one of my neighbors in the supermarket, and while we were comparing meats, he blurts out, "Joy, I just want you to know that I voted for Trump because Hillary and Obama want to take my guns away. I need them for protection!" I was stunned; I dropped my chicken thighs and said, "David, nobody is taking your guns away. Obama was in office for eight years. You still have your guns, right? And Hillary didn't want to take away *your* guns, she wanted to take away guns from people who shouldn't have them. And as for protection, you have three shotguns, a pistol, and an AK-47. How much protection do you need? You live in the city, not the Sudan. Who do you think is coming after you, Girl Scouts during cookie season? I assure you, Little Mindy isn't going to pull a Glock if you don't buy a box of Thin Mints."

I don't know why today's Republicans are so fascinated by weapons. I miss the good old days, when all the Republicans cared about was saving money and wearing dowdy clothes.

The GOP base is constantly yelling, "Second Amendment, Second Amendment, Second Amendment!" as though they've actually read the Constitution. (And why should they? It's not like their leader has, or even can.) Pardon the pun, but all they know are the bullet points of the Second Amendment because they've heard some right-wing nut ranting about it on the radio.

And it's not just standard firearms they think they should be allowed to have. They think the Second Amendment gives them the right to have *any* kind of weapon they want. Why stop at assault rifles? Why not have howitzers and bazookas and cannons in the garage? How about a couple of tanks or an atomic bomb in the backyard? Maybe a nuclear submarine in the pool?

Republicans love saying, "Guns don't kill people, people kill people." I beg to differ. If guns don't kill people, why do we give our soldiers guns rather than spatulas?

After the horrible school shootings in Newtown, Connecticut, at first the pro-gun contingent suggested that the teachers should be armed. Really? I was once a teacher. Forget about giving me a handgun. I had trouble working a staple gun. Terrible idea.

So, then the Republicans said we should just keep the guns out of the hands of the mentally ill and everything will be okay. This assumes that just because you haven't been diagnosed means that you're not mentally ill. Look around you. Does that sound reasonable to assume? Where I grew up, between the cat lady, the neighborhood flasher, and the guy who used to say, "Good morning, Ted," to the fire hydrant, there were plenty of people with undiagnosed illnesses. But even if you say that only the mentally ill should not have guns, why, in February 2017, did the House GOP block a measure that would have prevented the mentally ill from getting firearms? You tell me who's crazy . . .

P.S. If we didn't have guns, when Trump's sons went hunting, they'd have to strangle the lions. Now, *that's* a fight I'd pay to watch.

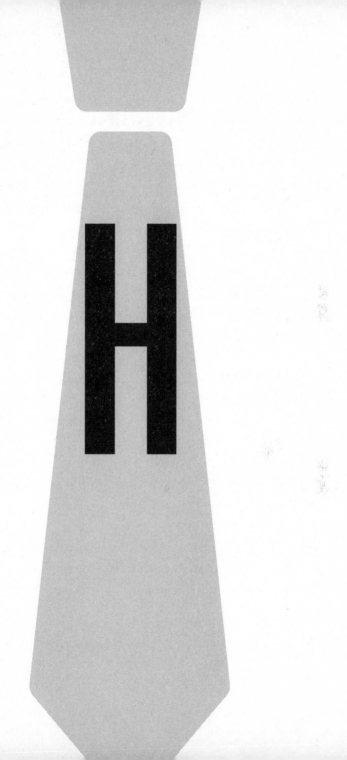

H **is for Hair.** I was born with naturally frizzy hair. For me to look the way I look on television requires curlers, straighteners, blow dryers, keratin, and a SWAT team. But when the cameras roll . . . *c'est magnifique!* Which is why I have trouble reconciling the situation on top of Donald Trump's head. He clearly spends a lot of time getting it organized, and the process appears to involve tape, glue, pins, gel, spray, staples, nails, and industrial-grade rivets. Yet, when the cameras roll . . . *mucho ridiculoso.* As we learned on *The Apprentice,* Trump loves firing people. My suggestion? He should fire not only whoever does his hair, but whoever he has on payroll telling him it looks good.

To be fair, it's not a Trump family problem. The problem is *his* hair. The others have terrific tresses. His wife . . . er, I mean, his *wives* all have great hair. Ivana, Marla, and Melania? Not a split end in sight. The daughters, Ivanka and Tiffany? Silky and smooth. And underneath the gel and mousse, Hans and Fritz have normal heads of hair. Even the little one, Barron, comes out of Supercuts looking good. The Hair Horror belongs solely to Herr Trump.

(FYI: I'm not a big fan of making fun of people's looks, but since Trump and his acolytes have no problem mocking the disabled, denigrating women, and their alleged plastic surgery I'm making an exception.)

H **is for Hans and Fritz.** Hans and Fritz are my nicknames for Trump's two eldest sons, Donald Jr. and Eric. They're the winners of my Most Annoying Siblings in History Contest, an amazing achievement considering the competition: Lyle and Erik Menendez, Donny and Marie, the Olsen twins, two-thirds of the Duggars, and Cain and Abel.

I know what you're thinking: "Seriously, Joy? Cain and Abel?" Yes. To me, those two are less annoying than Hans and Fritz, if for no other reason than that they supported themselves and didn't mooch off their parents. (Adam and Eve's parenting skills are a conversation for another book.)

I could handle Hans and Fritz's smugness and hair gel, but when I saw the photos of them hunting wild animals, I lost it. There they were, in Africa, smiling from ear to ear, proudly displaying the body of a defenseless leopard they had gunned down. I was disgusted but not surprised. Why wouldn't those two go after big cats? It's a family tradition: their father grabs pussies, doesn't he?

is for **Hypocrisy**. Other than acid reflux, mimes, and people whose dentures click when they chew, nothing bothers me more than hypocrisy.

H **is for Harvard**. The school that President Obama attended . . . and Donald Trump didn't. Nah nah nah nah nah!

H **is for Hawaii**. Or, as Donald Trump thinks of it, Kenya Adjacent.

H is for Health Care. Until recently, whenever a politician used the words *health care*, I'd fall asleep. A glass of wine and five minutes of Debbie Wasserman Schultz on C-SPAN, and I'm out like Sunny von Bülow at a slumber party.

Democrats have been talking about health care for thirty years. And for thirty years, Republican voters have ignored them and independent voters have dozed off. It's a boring topic—important, but boring. Dems use terms like *policies* and *premiums* and *copays*, and have to fight for attention. Republicans use terms like *death panels* and *government control*, and they have their voters frothing at the mouth like rabid dogs.

So, how, you ask, did President Obama get the Affordable Care Act passed? Easy. Just like in comedy, the answer is timing: right place, right time. When Obama took office, the baby boomers had just started hitting retirement age, and suddenly every politician had constituents with preexisting conditions or with twenty-something kids who needed to stay on their parents' insurance plans. For Democrats, it was a boon; for Republicans, it was a perfect storm. The Affordable Care Act was exactly that—an affordable care act. But since that sounded good, the Republicans referred to it as "Obamacare," so it would sound bad, because they had decided that anything the "Kenyan socialist" did was bad.

But now that the "Kenyan socialist" has been replaced by a rich sociopath, it's safe for Republicans to repeal and replace the Affordable Care Act with a plan of their own—a plan that will offer less help to fewer people and give more money to more companies and huge tax breaks to the rich. They can't decide if they should call their plan "Trumpcare" or "Ryan-care." I think they should call it exactly what it is: "Dying is easy. Health care is hard."

H **is for Hero.** During the campaign, Donald Trump said that John McCain wasn't a war hero because he'd been captured, "and I like people who weren't captured, okay?" The truth is, McCain withstood unbearable torture for his country. I'm not talking about his five years in the Hanoi Hilton. I'm talking about his two months on the campaign bus with Sarah Palin. Talk about torture. I'd rather be waterboarded.

Donald Trump is the last person in America who should be questioning John McCain's courage. Trump avoided the draft the way Mel Gibson avoids Passover Seders. Our commander in chief got five deferments to avoid serving in Vietnam, one of them because he had a sore foot. (He probably hurt it step-ping on one of his employees.) Trump also said that when he was younger he had such a busy sex life that "avoiding STDs was his Vietnam."

Wow. Maybe one of our Wounded Warriors could point out that there's a big difference between getting blown up and get-ting blown.

H **is for Hillary Hypocrisy.** Nowhere was Trump's hypoc-risy on display more than on the campaign trail. Trump dumped more crap on the trail than Seabiscuit at Belmont. He kept accusing Hillary of things he himself was actually doing. Here's a small tasting menu of his hypocritical hors d'oeuvres:

- Trump accused Hillary of being a bigot. Trump says he's the "least racist person you'll ever meet." And if you don't believe him, feel free to ask the eleven million nonwhite people he plans on deporting.

- During the campaign, Trump said Hillary "never talked about policy." That's *all* she's ever talked about. At her wedding, when the minister asked her, "Do you take this man to be your lawfully wedded husband?" she said, "As per page nineteen, clause seven, of the amendment to the rider to the original proposal . . . I do." Meanwhile, Trump's idea of a policy statement is "Believe me."

- Trump has accused Hillary of being "involved with Russia." If he meant that she once gave a lap dance to Boris Yeltsin, then, okay, fine. But when Trump cuts himself shaving, vodka comes out.

- Trump said that Hillary "does not have the temperament to be president." Yet, in the past few months alone, he's picked fights with Mexico, Britain, China, Australia, France, Greece, Canada, the CIA, the FBI, the NSA, the United Nations, NATO, *SNL*, the handicapped, Rosie O'Donnell, Robert De Niro, Meryl Streep, and the Freedom Caucus, a.k.a. the Tea Party.

H is for Hindenburg. The most famous blimp disaster in New Jersey that didn't involve shutting down lanes on the George Washington Bridge.

H **is for History.** "Those who don't know history are doomed to repeat it." Variations of this quote have been attributed to many people, including Edmund Burke, George Santayana (often confused with Carlos Santana), Winston Churchill, and the guy who lives next door to me, who's caught his hand in his car door so many times he's changed his name from Elliott to "Lefty." Considering that Donald Trump knows nothing of history, I'd like to recommend the following reading material before it's too late: *The Rise and Fall of the Roman Empire* (for where the country is headed), *All the President's Men* (for where *he's* headed), and *Working on the Chain Gang* (for where his surrogates are headed).

H **is for Homosexual.** Which is who Donald Trump should hire to fix his fucking hair. Do you think any sighted gay man would let him go out looking like that? Of course not. Even a blind gay man could feel Trump's head and say, "Oh no, sister! You are not leaving this Oval Office until someone with a brush or a wand works some magic on you." And let me add that since the "party" will probably start chipping away at LGBTQ rights, the chances of his mop ever, ever improving are becoming close to nil. And who suffers for that? You and me, my dears. You and me because we have to look at it for as long as it takes to impeach this guy.

H **is for Humorless.** Critics make fun of Hillary Clinton's laugh, saying it's more a cackle than a laugh. Well, at least she has a sense of humor—to this day, the woman can't walk past a cigar shop without giggling.

Donald Trump, on the other hand, almost never laughs. He's been roasted by the Friars Club and Comedy Central, he's hosted *Saturday Night Live*, and he's attended White House Correspondents' Dinners, yet I've never seen him laugh, not once. What are the odds that at shows like that, put on by the nation's best comedians and writers, not *one* thing has ever been written or said that was even marginally amusing to him?

I'm a comedian. I've done stand-up for thirty years. And in all that time, both onstage and off, I've never met anyone who doesn't like to laugh or have a good time. Even Hitler knew how to have a good time. Check out this pic of Adolf dancing a

Universal History Archive/Getty Images

jig with Goering at Berchtesgaden. Is it too much to ask to see a photo of Trump and Bannon twerking at Mar-a-Lago?

There are various explanations for Trump's seeming inability to laugh. A shrink friend of mine says that "laughter relieves shame," and since Trump has no shame (see: *Shame*), he has nothing to relieve, so this theory makes perfect sense. In 2012, a social anthropologist and an evolutionary biologist wrote a paper stating that people who don't laugh practice self-deception, and self-deception leads to inflated ego and outsize self-esteem. And since Trump lies to everybody, including himself, and is a world-class narcissist, this is a definite possibility. If Trump laughed, he would be responding to something funny *someone else* did or said, and that would make the laughter about them, not him, so he's unable to do it.

I'm not a shrink, but I have my own theory on the highly important subject of why POTUS is such a sourpuss. I believe that The Donald: (a) might be too dumb to get the jokes; (b) is afraid he won't get the jokes, and he'd rather look like a scowling menace than a feckless dunce; or (c) won't admit that someone else is getting attention and applause.

H is for Hyperbole. In a previous entry, I put Trump's sons in the same category as Donny and Marie. Clearly, that's hyperbolic exaggeration—Donny and Marie actually smiled (boy, did they smile). I don't think Hans and Fritz have ever smiled. I think they got the antismiling gene from their humorless father. But I'm a comedian writing a satirical book, not the leader of the free world. If I grossly exaggerate something, it's just a joke. My words won't make Syrian refugees turn around and head back to Damascus, or make Dumb Jong-un in North Korea fire off nuclear missiles. The worst that'll happen is that someone won't laugh and someone else will go online and say, "Joy Behar's a moron." (Like I haven't heard that before! Okay, I hear it every day, but usually it's from people who actually know me.)

The point is Donald Trump *always* speaks in hyperbole: everything is a disaster or carnage or a failure—rhetoric that can be dangerous, because he's the president. When he speaks like that, it paints a false picture of reality. It helped him get elected, of course, but it could also lead to serious international trouble. I don't want Iceland invading Bermuda because of some 5:00 a.m. tweet in which Trump claimed that thousands of Bermudans were laughing about exploding lava fields near Reykjavík.

H **is for Hypocrisy.** Other than acid reflux, mimes, and people whose dentures click when they chew, nothing bothers me more than hypocrisy—or, as I like to think of it, the Republican way of life.

Okay, class, let's start at the top of the recent hypocrisy list and work our way down:

- In 2012, Citizen Trump criticized presidential candidate Mitt Romney for not releasing his tax returns. President Trump still refuses to release his tax returns.

- In 2016, Candidate Trump said, "Hedge fund guys are getting away with murder." President Trump appointed a hedge fund guy to be treasury secretary.

- President Trump, who didn't go to public schools, nominated a woman, Betsy DeVos, who didn't go to public schools and who doesn't believe in public schools, to be secretary of education.

- Professional Christian and all-around homophobe Mike Pence accused mothers who put their kids in daycare of having "stunted emotional growth." He then voted *against* paid family leave.

- In 2012, Mitch McConnell, the Concubine of Coal, wrote a bill about the debt ceiling. As soon as President Obama agreed to sign it, Murky Mitch decided to filibuster his own bill.

And what of the GOP It-boy, Paul Ryan? I've never seen Paul Ryan's balls, and I don't want to, but I'll bet they're huge. The smarmy Speaker once announced publicly that repealing Obamacare was "an act of mercy." Really? Is there anything less merciful than letting poor, sick families suffer? Ryan doesn't think so. He probably believes that if, God forbid, the Gosselins, the Duggars, and Octomom all lost their health insurance, got sick, and died at the exact same time, such acts of mercy might get him nominated for sainthood. It could happen; Paulie's already performed at least two miracles: (1) he's convinced voters that his destructive policies are good for them, and (2) he's managed to spend time alone with Donald Trump without drinking, throwing up, or jumping off the roof of the South Portico. One more highly unlikely achievement and Ryan will end up either being canonized by the Pope or joining the R&B group Smokey Robinson and the Miracles.

H **is for Hysteria.** Conservative pundits and the right-wing media keep saying that liberals like me are engaged in hysteria over Trump's election. They're wrong. I'm not hysterical; I'm horrified. Hysterical is what I am when the woman in front of me at Saks gets the last pair of Junior Petite Spanx. Horrified is what I am when crazy people take charge of the country. Big difference.

is for Ignorance. The old saying "Ignorance is bliss" is absolutely true—for the person who's ignorant. Everyone else is screwed. And if the ignorant person is in charge of everyone else, it's not bliss; it's bedlam.

Donald Trump isn't just ignorant, he's aggressively ignorant. Proudly ignorant. He wears his ignorance like a merit badge. But he's not alone. Ignorance is a Republican tradition, like flag waving and wearing cotton-poly blends. James Inhofe, Steven King, Louis Gohmert, Sarah Palin . . . shall I go on? Sarah Palin thinks dinosaurs roamed the earth in 1957. Unless she's referring to Strom Thurmond, she'd better check with a paleontologist.

is for Immigrant. The following people are/were immigrants to the United States:

Donald Trump's grandfather

Donald Trump's grandmother

Donald Trump's first wife

Donald Trump's third wife

Jared Kushner's grandmother

Albert Einstein

Madeleine Albright

Joseph Pulitzer

Enrico Fermi

Irving Berlin

Alex Trebek

Eight of the signers of the Constitution

William Penn

Alexander Hamilton

The Pilgrims

Christopher Columbus . . .

. . . and the most important of all . . .
Dr. Ruth.

Can you imagine how much crankier Republicans would be if they *weren't* having good sex?

is for Incidental Contact. I think of incidental contact the same way I think of diabetes—there are two types:

Type 1: You're getting ready to cross the street and you break a heel of your shoe on the handicapped ramp and bump into the person in the wheelchair in front of you. This is incidental contact—unless you knock the person into oncoming traffic, in which case it's no longer incidental contact; it's involuntary manslaughter.

Type 2: You brush up against somebody and you like it so much that, twenty minutes later, you need a cigarette and a shower. When this type of incidental contact happens on New York City subways, it's called "frottage," which comes from the French word *frotter*, which means "to rub against a stranger." To some people, it may be a prelude to pussy-grabbing. I've been on crowded subways a million times and not once have I ever been groped, grabbed, or fondled. Then again, I've never been on the subway with Donald Trump or Bill O'Reilly.

is for Incomprehensible Demoralization. One of my Twelve Step friends—I work in television; it's a union rule that everyone who works in show business has to have *at least* three friends in rehab, two in AA, and one with an electronic ankle bracelet and live-in sobriety coach—tells me that when addicts and alcoholics reach their bottom, one of the things they deal with is the feeling of incomprehensible demoralization. I've had that feeling since the 2016 election. Does this mean that in order to get over it, I have to start drinking like an alcoholic? If so, I'd better stop writing and run to 7-Eleven for a six-pack of Schlitz.

is for India. Trump keeps saying he's going to bring jobs back to America from foreign countries. Manufacturing? Technology? Not likely. Call centers, perhaps? That would be a huge gain. When is the last time you called a customer service department or an airline and spoke to someone who wasn't living in Mumbai? So, is Donald #ImmigrantsBad Trump planning on bringing 3.2 million Indian workers here? And if so, would he have to lift his own travel ban to do so?

Slightly off point, but why do the call centers make the operators take on American names? You call to make a flight reservation, and you hear a man say, in a very thick Hindi accent, "Hello, this is Kevin, can I help you?" It's ridiculous. I know his name's not Kevin, and *he* knows I know his name's not Kevin, and I know he knows I know his name's not Kevin, so what's the point? I'm perfectly happy speaking with Vijay or Lakshmi or Subramanian. Just get me a friggin' aisle seat on American Airlines.

If Trump really wants to bring American jobs back home, maybe he should stop making his ties and suits in China (and Ivanka should stop making her clothes in Hong Kong and Vietnam) and open factories here. (And maybe Hans and Fritz should stop killing elephants in Africa and go on safaris in New York City and shoot the rats in the basement of Trump Tower.)

is for Insomnia. Lack of sleep can lead to physical, psychological, and emotional problems. In my case, it can lead to five extra pounds, because if I'm awake at three o'clock in the morning, so is my refrigerator. According to *Psychology Today*, lack of sleep can lead to impaired brain activity, disorganized thoughts,

is for **Iran**. Forget a nuclear holocaust— if Trump screws things up with Iran, how will I be able to buy Persian rugs? I have my priorities.

cognitive dysfunction, moodiness, memory problems, and bursts of irrationality. Apparently, it can also lead to insane tweeting in the middle of the night.

It's possible that Trump's biggest problem is that he hasn't slept since 1997. Have you seen what time he likes to tweet? Maybe all the man needs is a good nap. Can you imagine if all we needed to fix this hot mess were a prescription for Ambien? (Our luck, he'd be one of those rare people who experience side effects from Ambien. Some people unconsciously sleepwalk, others mow the lawn or make a meatloaf. He'd probably drop a bomb on Canada.)

is for Intolerant. The opposite of *intolerant* is *tolerant*. I hate those words. *Tolerant* means you're willing to grudgingly put up with something. Teenagers are professional tolerators. They are amazingly skilled at rolling their eyes, shrugging their shoulders, and making sucking sounds with their teeth to express their disgust. (Or is that just me on *The View*?) Whenever asked to do something, they do it grudgingly, if at all. This is typical teenage behavior, not a national political party platform. Most teenagers outgrow it, but apparently the GOP has not.

After Obama beat Romney in 2012, the Republican leadership decided they needed to appear more "tolerant" of minorities, gays, and other people who don't usually vote for them. Who are they to "tolerate" anybody? You tolerate lactose or barking dogs or the unexplained success of Sean Hannity—you don't "tolerate" people just because they don't contribute money to your PAC.

The minute a minority group gains some rights, Republicans send Rick Santorum or Mike Pence to the grave of Jesse Helms to suck some meanness out of his bones to infuse back into the party.

(I have to stop writing this entry. It's making me crazy. I just can't tolerate intolerance.)

is for Iran. During the campaign, Donald Trump said that the Iran nuclear deal President Obama had signed was "a horrible deal; disastrous." He must have meant it was a bad deal for him, because he wasn't making any money off it. The Iran nuclear deal was signed by the five permanent members of the UN Security Council—China, France, Russia, the United States, and the United Kingdom—*and* the European Union. Mathematically, what are the odds that every single one of these nations was duped into making the same terrible deal, but that a reality TV show host knows better? I'm not an arms expert, nor do I play one on TV, but I think we have to keep the Iran deal in place. Forget a nuclear holocaust—if Trump screws things up with Iran, how will I be able to buy Persian rugs? I have my priorities.

is for Iraq. There are only a handful of people who think that invading Iraq in 2003 was a good idea: Dick Cheney, George W. Bush, Dick Cheney, Donald Rumsfeld, and Dick Cheney—oh, and whoever is profiting off the war and occupation—probably a certain person who is related to Betsy DeVos.

We've been in Iraq for almost fifteen years, and we don't

seem to be leaving it anytime soon. In fact, Trump's just requested an increase in troops and funding. It's no longer an occupation; we've moved in. Time to redecorate. I have a bunch of 20 percent–off coupons from Bed, Bath & Beyond. Where do I send them?

is for IRS. Trump says he wants to rewrite the tax code. I don't believe that for a second. He doesn't pay his taxes now, why would he change anything?

is for Israel. Israel has always been one of America's strongest allies. This is important to me because, my whole life, I've always gone out with Jewish guys and I'm married to a Jewish guy.

I know that not everyone who lives in Israel is Jewish (in the same way I know that not everyone who lives in the Keebler Forest is an elf), but it *was* created as a Jewish state. There are different reasons that everyone in America—and every U.S. president—cares about Israel. For some evangelicals, it has to do with the Rapture. (According to the New Testament's Book of Revelation, after the Battle of Armageddon, Jesus will take all believers up to heaven, and all nonbelievers—I wonder who they could be—will, *poof*, like magic, be gone.) For others, it's because Israel's the only democracy in the Middle East; for still others, it's because Israel is our eyes and ears on the ground in the region. Republicans ranted and raved that Obama didn't like Israel because he and Bibi Netanyahu didn't get along. They didn't get along because Obama is a center-left conciliator and Netanyahu is a right-wing hawk. Trump likes Israel, too, but for a completely different reason, and I don't think it's because the Kushners are Jewish, or because he loves gefilte fish. I think it's because he's having a bromance with Bibi—if for no other reason than to make his main squeeze, Vladimir, jealous. Either way, it doesn't sound kosher to me.

is for Ivana. Ivana Zelnickova was the first woman to say, "I do," to Donald Trump. Of course, she said it in Czech, so who the hell knows what she really said? It could have been, "Shove that prenup up your ass, you orange-hued motherfucker. In a couple of years, I'll have half of everything you own." I'm not sure how they met—maybe she was starring on *Prague's Got Talent* or the sitcom *Hot in Ostrava*—but they had a whirlwind romance and a huge wedding in New York City. They had a few kids, and everything was going fine until, one day, The Donald decided to play Hide the Kielbasa with Marla Maples. He cheated on Ivana publicly, and faster than you can say, "Don't get mad, get everything," she filed for divorce. She reportedly walked away with twenty million bucks and, because she's the only woman he seems intimidated by or afraid of, I'm guessing pictures of Donald in a compromising position (like blow-drying his hair). You go, girl!

is for Ivanka Danka-Doo. Ivanka Trump is America's youngest First Lady. I know, technically she's not the First Lady, but she *is* the only woman related to Donald Trump who has an office in the West Wing. His actual wife has an office on QVC and sleeps in Trump Tower whenever she can get away

[Merkel] I am the chancellor of Germany, I was a
research scientist, and I have a doctorate in physical
science.
[Ivanka] My father thinks you're a two.

from DC and DT. Now that Melania has moved into the White
House, will she be known as the First Lady or, because she's
his third wife, as the Third Lady? Or should we call her the
First Trophy? It's very confusing.

I don't know Ivanka Trump. She seems smart and composed
and poised. Of course, compared to her father, the guy from
the movie *Jackass* seems smart and composed and poised.

Is it just me, or do the daughters of most Republican presidents seem smarter than their fathers? Jenna and Barbara Bush are clearly smarter than W. (Although, truth be told, I don't think the bar was set too high for them.) Patti Davis? Definitely brighter than Ronnie. Was Susan Ford smarter than Gerald Ford? Duh. Even the Nixon girls might have been smarter than their dad. At least Tricia knew enough to shave off her five o'clock shadow before going on television.

Ivanka Trump grew up in the public eye, so fame is nothing new for her. She started out as a model and appeared in lots of fashion magazines and runway shows. I'm not sure if she was a model or a "supermodel." I don't really know the difference. Do supermodels leap tall salad bars in a single bound, or pop laxatives with the speed of a locomotive?

Ivanka went to Georgetown for two years, then transferred to the Wharton School of Business, where she graduated cum laude. (The Donald also went to Wharton, and even though he can't stop telling us how smart he is, he didn't graduate with honors, he didn't get an MBA, and he may have gotten in only due to familial influence and wealth.) Ivanka took what she learned at Wharton and brought it to the business world. She's lucky she didn't go to Trump University; she'd have brought what she learned there into an unemployment office or a courtroom.

Ivanka's having an MBA from Wharton definitely makes her qualified to run a business—but to negotiate international trade agreements with Angela Merkel? I don't think so. How much do you think the Republicans would have carried on if

President Obama had sent Malia to Cuba to renegotiate the embargo with Raúl Castro?

White House "insiders" say Ivanka has her father's ear, and he'll actually listen to her every now and again. (And by "insiders," I mean the people who haven't been fired yet because they forgot to compliment Donald.) Apparently, Ivanka can talk her father out of following his worst instincts. And considering the mess he's already created, can you imagine what she's talked him out of?

Things Ivanka Has Talked Her Father Out Of

- Referring to British prime minister Theresa May as the Brexit Babe;

- Drilling for oil in Johnny Depp's hair;

- Selling Hawaii to Kenya;

- Naming Bruno Mars the head of NASA;

- Giving a Kennedy Center Honor to Chachi;

- Changing "Stop and Frisk" to "Stop and Punch in the Fucking Face"; and

- Building a wall around Rosie O'Donnell's house.

J is for Andrew Jackson. Steve Bannon, Newt Gingrich, and Rudy Giuliani—and they wonder why women WANT to become lesbians—have all compared Donald Trump to Andrew Jackson. The Donald must be so proud. While there *are* some similarities (they both ran as outsiders and as populists), Jackson was a statesman while Trump is . . . actually, I don't know what the fuck Donald Trump is, but he's definitely not a statesman. Trump has more in common with Michael Jackson than Andrew Jackson. Michael Jackson had clingy, leechy adult siblings; Donald Trump has clingy, leechy adult children. Michael's hair caught fire; Donald has a warning sign on his comb-over that reads, DANGER: HIGHLY FLAMMABLE.

Want a fabulous irony? Andrew Jackson's nickname was Stonewall, which is also the name of the New York City bar where the gay rights movement started, a bar where I'll bet some of today's most homophobic Republican lawmakers would love to loiter.

J is for Jared-of-all-Trades. When speaking about his son-in-law, Jared Kushner, Donald Trump turns into a reverse Sally Field—"I like him, I really, really like him!" (And I say "like," not "love," because the only person, place, or thing Donald Trump truly loves is Donald Trump.)

I'm not sure if The Donald likes The Jared because he is the scion of a rich New York City family, because he went to a good school, or because he's sleeping with Ivanka (and we all know how much Daddy loves Ivanka). Regardless, Kushner has enormous power in the White House.

Jared's White House duties—none of which he's qualified to perform—include the following: negotiating peace in
the Middle East; heading the White House Office of American Innovation; modernizing the Department of Veterans'
Affairs; assisting Chris Christie in solving the opioid crisis;
reforming the criminal justice system; serving as a liaison to
Mexico; serving as a liaison to China; and serving as a liaison
to the Muslim community—because who better to smooth over
Trump's xenophobic, anti-Muslim rhetoric than an Orthodox
Jew? That's like sending Sean Hannity to run Al Franken's
campaign.

You must be thinking, "Is there anything Jared Kushner
can't do?" The answer is he can do anything and everything!
The man wears more hats than conjoined septuplets. My
sources tell me that Daddy-in-Law-Dearest has quietly given
Jared lots of other responsibilities, in addition to the ones I've
just listed. Here are a few of them:

- Recovering lost gold from the *Titanic* and the *Lusitania*;
- Taking over as lead male dancer for the American Ballet The-
atre;
- Chairing a new Republican activist group, Black Lives Sorta
Matter;
- Explaining to his father-in-law why the Holocaust was bad;
- Playing shortstop for the New York Yankees;
- Serving as head of Cardiology at Mount Sinai Hospital;

- Locking up Hillary Clinton with James Comey;
- Getting Ivanka's handbags and belts back into Nordstrom; and
- Changing the name of the White House to Don-a-Lago.

J is for **jellyfish**. A jellyfish is a dangerous spineless creature that can cause severe and debilitating pain in unsuspecting innocent people. Sorry—my mistake. That's not a jellyfish, that's Mitch McConnell.

J is for Jazz. I feel about jazz the way I feel about moderate, normal Republicans who voted for Donald Trump. I want to understand and I want to like them more than I do, but I'm completely baffled by the whole thing. At least with jazz, you're usually listening to it in a hip club with a cocktail in your hand. How do you sit down and drink with people who agree with Ben Carson that the pyramids were used to store grain (did King Tut know this?), that dinosaurs roamed the Earth along with people (maybe just Strom Thurmond?), and that Satan walks among us (Dick Cheney is still alive)? Maybe there's hope yet to sit down with more moderate Republicans, if you can find any. Maybe they're hiding in the pyramids with the grain?

J is for Jefferson Beauregard Sessions. At one point in 2017, Attorney General Sessions said, "I am really amazed that a judge sitting on an island in the Pacific can issue an order that stops the president of the United States from what appears to be clearly his statutory and constitutional power." By "island in the Pacific," Sessions was referring to Hawaii. Excuse me? *Guam* is an island in the Pacific; *Tahiti* is an island in the Pacific; *Bora Bora* (named for Charles Krauthammer) is an island in the Pacific. Hawaii has been the fiftieth U.S. state since 1959, and the *real* birthplace of the last president of the United States—you know, the one who *doesn't* Snapchat with Vladimir Putin.

Jeff Sessions is from Alabama, a state that in 2014 was ranked forty-seventh in education—the third worst in the nation, beating only Mississippi and the District of Columbia. (It somehow edged out Louisiana.) Poor little Jeff Sessions, who was thirteen in 1959, never got the lesson that Hawaii became a state. And here he is today, with the same lack of knowledge about the country that he claims to love so much. Maybe he needs to start watching cable TV like his boss, so he can learn something. But, not to worry. I'm sure our brilliant secretary of education, the woman whose brain is always in reverse, Betsy Devour, will straighten him out at the next Cabinet meeting. I hope she's wearing a lei.

J is for Jellyfish. A jellyfish is a dangerous spineless creature that can cause severe and debilitating pain in unsuspecting innocent people. Oh no, I'm sorry. My mistake. That's not a jellyfish. That's Mitch McConnell.

J **is for Jerusalem.** One of Trump's first suggestions as president was that the U.S. embassy in Israel be moved from Tel Aviv to Jerusalem, because why leave well enough alone when you have the opportunity to create chaos, division, and religious resentment in one of the most violent and volatile regions in the world? Why? I'm guessing because there's a possibility of building a Trump Tower in Jerusalem, that's why.

J **is for Jesus.** This is a very tough one for Trump. When someone asks him about Jesus, he doesn't know whether to suck up to his evangelical base or deport his gardener.

J **is for JFK.** The president, not the airport. In 1963, President Kennedy, who, by the way, won a close election without the help of the Russians or James Comey (although a call from mobster Sam Giancana didn't hurt) went to Berlin to speak about democracy and freedom as counterpoints to communism. This was shortly after the Berlin Wall had been erected (and I must say, it was quite an erection). A few great quotes came out of that speech—which Kennedy delivered in full sentences, never once using the words *bigly*, *best*, or *pussy*. Kennedy had two main talking points in the speech: freedom and unity. He talked about the wall that separates families and divides countrymen; he praised the mayor of West Berlin and the chancellor of West Germany; and his most famous quote was: "Two thousand years ago, the proudest boast was 'civis Romanus sum' [I am a Roman citizen]. Today, in the world of freedom, the proudest boast is 'Ich bin ein Berliner!' . . . All free men, wherever they may live, are citizens of Berlin. And, therefore, as a free man, I take pride in the words 'Ich bin ein Berliner!'" (We'll ignore the fact that *Ich bin ein Berliner* literally means "I am a donut.")

Fifty-four years later, we have a president who says, "We're going to build that wall, and Mexico is going to pay for it"—which is, of course, ridiculous. Mexico is not going to pay for any wall; if there's going to be a wall, we'll have to build it and pay for it. The good news? Given Trump's history of stiffing contractors, it's quite possible that no one will pay for it—it will end up in bankruptcy court. How fabulous would it be to see the Orange Amigo ending up on the wrong side of the wall, standing in Tijuana, yelling, "Ich bin ein Mexicano"? Will he even realize they speak Spanish in Mexico?

J is for Jimmy Hoffa. Mobbed-up Teamsters leader Jimmy Hoffa vanished in 1975. He went to meet a "friend" at a restaurant outside Detroit and was never seen again. (How bad could the food have been?) Seriously, his disappearance is one of the great mysteries of the world, along with the building of the pyramids, the Shroud of Turin, and why the white tiger ate Roy but didn't so much as lick Siegfried. Every few years, someone comes up with a new theory as to where Jimmy Hoffa is buried. One theory is that he was under the end zone in the old Giants' Stadium in the swamps of New Jersey's Meadowlands. (My husband says if that's true, he would have been found years ago, if only the Giants had scored more often.) Another story goes that his body was thrown into the Florida

Everglades, where it was probably eaten by alligators. My theory is that it doesn't matter: we'll never, ever find Jimmy Hoffa's body because he was buried in a coffin along with Donald Trump's tax returns.

J **is for Job**. These days the poor thing is a total wreck. Even he can't take the constant drama. He's had to stop watching Rachel Maddow and Keith Olbermann, he's cancelled his *New York Times* subscription, and he's deleted the *Huffington Post* app from his iPhone. Since November 8, Job has been living on Xanax and vodka. If Job, the most patient guy in history besides Wolf Blitzer, can't take it, how do you think the rest of us feel?

J **is for Job Application.** We've all filled out job applications, and we've all fudged a little bit. For example, years ago, before I got into show business, I applied for a job as a receptionist at ABC. I fudged my résumé a little. Where it asked for "previous experience," I put down, "Translator at the UN." That wasn't exactly true—what *was* true was that I once yelled at a Croatian cab driver for slamming on the brakes and almost knocking my teeth out. I thought he didn't speak English, so I gave him the finger, which he clearly understood. He told me to fuck off. Voilà! International translator!

Anyway, I got the job at ABC. (It didn't last long; they fired me—something about my having a "bad attitude." Who, *moi*?) But if you want a job in the Trump administration, is lying on your application a bad thing or a requirement?

TRUMP ADMINISTRATION
JOB APPLICATION

Name _____

  Alias _____

  LLC Name _____

  Bogus LLC Name _____

Legal Address _____

  Illegal Address _____

  Bank Address _____

  Offshore Bank Address _____

  Offshore Shell Company Bank Address

  _____

Name(s) of Lawyer(s) _____

  Name(s) of Bankruptcy Lawyer(s)

  _____

Previous Nonrelated Job Experience

  _____

  _____

If Hillary Clinton were on fire, I would:

    a. Put her out

    b. Call 9–1–1

    c. Ignore her

    d. Pee on her

If Donald Trump were on fire, I would:

    a. Put him out

    b. Call 9–1–1

    c. Lock Hillary Clinton up

    d. Pee on him (he would like that)

Keep your friends close and your enemies:

    a. Dead

    b. In your basement/crawl space

    c. In Russia

    d. I don't have enemies; everyone loves me.

_____ is next to Godliness:

    a. Great wealth

    b. A uuuuge brain

    c. Power

    d. A woman with big hooters

Have you read the Constitution?

    a. No

b. No

c. No

d. What's the Constitution?

Donald Trump won the popular vote by:

a. Three million votes

b. Three hundred million votes

c. Three billion votes

d. Too many votes to count, but close to a gazillion

How important is loyalty to the ~~king~~ leader?

a. Very important

b. All-consuming

c. It's everything

d. I'd give up my children for him

Which percentage of your children do you like?

a. 80 percent

b. 66 percent

c. 50 percent

d. Only the pretty ones

Should the Bible be replaced with *The Art of the Deal*?

a. Yes

b. Duh

c. What's the Bible?

d. We doesn't reed

Cabinet officials should come from:

a.   Right-wing think tanks
b.   Right-wing radio
c.   Right-wing websites
d.   TV shows that feature Omarosa

How many women have you grabbed?

a.   A lot
b.   To many too count
c.   A gazillion
d.   If you're famous, they let you

Please submit this form to:

Whoever is in charge of things at the White House this week
1600 Pennsylvania Avenue
Washington, DC
United States of Make America Great Again

J is for Joe Biden. In a 2017 *New York Times* interview, one of the few not totally insane Republican senators, Ben Sasse of Nebraska (who loathes Trump), said Joe Biden would've clobbered Trump in the general election. We'll never know, but he might be right. Joe Biden is like Sara Lee: nobody doesn't like him. Biden is one of those rare career politicians who is liked and respected by both parties and has been able to work across the aisle for years. He's a patriot, and his personal story is so compelling that even the most craven, cold-hearted Republicans have a soft spot for Joe. That said, I disagree with Ben Sasse. Yes, a lot of Republicans like Joe Biden, but they would never have voted for him for president, because two things about him render him unelectable to a certain tranche of Republican voters: he's qualified for the job and he's a Democrat.

J **is for Joe the Plumber.** The Republicans began their formal drive for the undereducated, bigoted, disenfranchised white voter in 2008, when they made "Joe the Plumber" their cartoonish mascot. Turns out he was the perfect choice.

For starters, he's a liar: (a) he was not a licensed plumber in the state of Ohio, and (b) his name isn't Joe; it's Sam. His full name is Samuel Joseph Wurzelbacher. (Maybe he uses his middle name instead of his first name. It's entirely possible, but kind of unusual, no? I don't remember anybody calling Richard Nixon "Milhous," or John Kennedy "Fitzgerald," or Dwight Eisenhower "Big Dave," do you?)

Secondly, he's a gun nut. After the horrible 2014 shootings in Isla Vista, California, Sam/Joe wrote an open letter to the parents of the kids who were killed in which he said, "[Y]our dead kids don't trump my constitutional rights . . . We still have the right to bear arms." Nice, huh? He's also made some "unusual" Holocaust references. In 2012, when Sam/Joe the Not-Actual-Plumber decided to run for Congress, he made a progun campaign video that claimed that "in 1939, Germany established gun control. From 1939 to 1945, six million Jews and seven million others unable to defend themselves were exterminated." Call me crazy, but I don't think the Luftwaffe, the SS, and the Third Panzer Division could have been stopped by Rivka wielding a pistol. And finally, while appearing at a political rally in Arizona, he said, "Put a damn fence on the border, go into Mexico, and start shooting."

Sam/Joe is not the kind of person Republicans want running for Congress—he's the kind of person they want running for president. He's a total crackpot, but he might actually be able to drain the swamp. Don't forget, he's a plumber (not!).

J is for John Gotti. Donald Trump made his fortune (at least the part of it his daddy didn't give him) in the real estate development business, building primarily hotels and casinos. Given the nature of the construction business, what are the odds Donald Trump never dealt with, worked with, associated with, or paid off any members of an organized crime family? (Although, truth be told, if Trump were seriously involved with organized crime, it would no longer be organized.) I wouldn't be surprised if, one morning, he wakes up with a horse's head in his bed. And why not? Melania wakes up every morning with a horse's ass in hers.

J is for the Joker. An evil, erratic, cartoonish villain with crazy hair and bizarre makeup. Recently moved from Gotham City to the White House.

K is for Kansas. In 2005, journalist Thomas Frank wrote the best-selling book *What's the Matter with Kansas?*, which takes a look at why the people of Kansas (and other states) lurch to the political right and vote against their own self-interest. For example, why vote against universal health care, why vote against public education, why vote against clean air and water, why vote for tax cuts for the one-percenters, and why identify with a rich orange guy from Queens?

I'd rather look at what's great about Kansas. First on my list: wheat. Kansas is the number one state in wheat production, and I love bread. Without bread, I'd have to eat corned beef and pastrami on tofu, and I don't see that happening in this lifetime (or the next, or the next, or the next one after that—I put that in just in case Shirley MacLaine is reading this book). Second, aviation manufacturing is a big industry in Kansas. Without it, we wouldn't have planes, and as much as I hate flying, it's much better than other kinds of schlepping. I get carsick just going the twenty blocks from my apartment to work. I can't imagine spending eighteen hours on a Greyhound from New York to Miami sitting next to Ratso Rizzo, who wasn't exactly known for good hygiene. And third, and most important, *The Wizard of Oz*. Without Kansas, there's no Dorothy; and without Dorothy, there's no Judy Garland; and without Judy Garland, there's no fabulous conversation with my fabulous gay friends at their fabulous gay dinner parties. Yes, we could talk about Bette versus Joan, or who was the best Dolly Levi on Broadway, or how it's possible that anyone could still think John Travolta is straight. But, ultimately, it would all come back to Judy Garland. As well it should. What can I say, I ♥ Kansas! Even if they did vote for Donald Trump.

K is for Kardashian. I love the Kardashians. Why? Because they're fascinating? Certainly not. I've interviewed them a number of times, on both *The View* and my show on HLN, and while they're all very nice, they don't make for scintillating interviews (although Khloe can be funny in a kind of "I drank a fifth of lunch today" kind of way). I love them because *they* are the actual biggest international stars of reality TV, *not* Donald Trump. If you doubt this, feel free to travel around the world and speak to girls everywhere, and see whom they'd rather be like, Kim Kardashian or Donald Trump. I rest my case.

The Kardashians got famous because Kim made a sex tape with a rap artist named Ray J and it was leaked all over the Internet. I haven't seen the tape, and I have no desire to. If I want to hear a reality star moaning, I'll watch Val Chmerkovskiy try to lift Sherri Shepherd on *Dancing with the Stars* (apologies to my girl Sherri).

K is for Kevorkian. You can't have a doctor pull the plug just because you're having a bad hair day, though if I were a judge I might pull the plug on anyone who showed up in court with a mullet.

Anyway, while the Kardashians themselves might not be interesting, their choice of spouses is fascinating. First of all, there's the interracial thing, which I love. They also marry athletes and celebrities: Kanye West, Kris Humphries, Lamar Odom, Bruce Jenner, and Robert Kardashian. When it comes to marriages, though, the family matriarch, Kris Jenner, is the bomb. Donald Trump may have married a few European beauty queens, but Kris married a lawyer who defended the world's most famous accused murderer (O.J. Simpson) and a famous athlete who became the world's most famous woman. Take that, loser!

K is for Dr. Kevorkian. In the 1990s, Dr. Jack Kevorkian became famous for promoting and practicing euthanasia on terminally ill patients (with their consent, of course; he didn't break into nursing homes and smother unsuspecting widows). Even though he went to jail, he made the issue of physician-assisted suicide part of the national conversation.

I think one of the reasons he got in trouble was his methodology. First, he advertised in local papers. "Fed up with coughing, sneezing, and wheezing? Sick and tired of being sick and tired? Call Dr. Jack and make a onetime appointment now. You'll never need a follow-up! Have your caregiver dial, 1–800–555-DEAD." Dr. Kevorkian also did some of his euthanasia work from inside his van, which became known as a Death Mobile. Even though I believe in physician-assisted suicide, dying in traffic is not for me. If I want to die in a van, I'll go for a ride with Barbara Walters. The woman is a menace behind the wheel. Was it my imagination, or did she try to run down Diane Sawyer on Madison Avenue once?

Five states (California, Colorado, Montana, Oregon, and Vermont) plus Washington, DC, have legalized physician-assisted suicide, passing legislation with names like the Death with Dignity Law. (I'm a big fan of death with dignity. No way do I want to be found in an undignified manner like David Carradine was: naked in a broom closet wearing a horse collar and chaps. I don't have the shoes for that.) The laws are stringent; you can't have a doctor pull the plug just because you're having a bad hair day—although, if I were a presiding judge, I might personally pull the plug on anyone who showed up in court with a mullet. Naturally, congressional Republicans, led by the always craven Jason Chaffetz, are against physician-assisted suicide. They do not believe in euthanasia. They think people should die naturally, you know, after getting sick with no health insurance, or by getting shot forty times by a mentally ill person with an assault rifle.

I think we should start calling this congressional-assisted suicide.

K **is for KKK Sera Sera.** During the 2016 campaign, Donald Trump received the endorsement of David Duke, the former leader of the KKK. Now, I don't even like being bothered by AARP let alone the KKK, and all AARP wants to do is sell me walk-in bathtubs and long-term-care insurance.

When Trump was asked about this dubious honor, at first he said he didn't know anything about David Duke (which, of course, wasn't true), but then, in response to criticism from both political parties, he disavowed the endorsement. A lot of people were annoyed that it took Trump so long to distance himself from Duke. I didn't care about that. What I care about is that Trump has never walked away from his belief system, which frighteningly aligns with David Duke's. They both champion nationalism, populism, and anti-immigrant stances; they traffic in outlandish conspiracy theories; and they're usually seen only in the company of white men. Trump may have disavowed Duke's endorsement publicly, but privately, I don't think the crabapple falls far from the tree.

K is for Korea. As Donald Trump would say, in his *elegant* way, South Korea good, North Korea bad; Donald Trump getting involved in either Korea, worse. Since the end of World War II, the United States and South Korea have been close allies, and when the Russian-backed North Koreans invaded the South in 1950, the United States (along with sixteen other UN member states) came to its aid. The United States and South Korea have been close economic, military, and cultural partners ever since. In 2013, President Obama cited the musical artist Psy's hit song "Gangnam Style" as part of South Korea's growing cultural influence. We returned the favor in 2016, with President PSYchotic's "Gangster Style" platform being cited as part of America's growing political craziness.

I don't love everything about Korean culture. For example, I've heard that they eat dogs. Somebody please get me Anthony Bourdain on the phone—I'd like him to verify whether in

Pyongyang a BLT is a "bacon, Lassie, and tomato." If true, I find this quite upsetting. I have no interest in eating Kung Pao Collie. If I go to South Korea, will I find chain restaurants like Kentucky Fried Corgi, or IHOP: International House of Poodles? I hope not, because unless Trump blows everything up, I might just go to South Korea. I'm not kidding. The 2018 Winter Olympics are in Pyeongchang, and while I care nothing about sports, I find the two-man luge kinda kinky.

K **is for Krispy Kreme.** I rarely see a very thin person walk out of a Krispy Kreme donut shop. (I'm not saying that only overweight people go there; it's entirely possible that chubbettes volunteer to go to the store for the whole family because they consider donut shopping exercise. Who am I to say?) But, to me, the consumption of Krispy Kremes is a metaphor for Donald Trump's hardcore base voters. They know they're buying something that, in the long run, may not be good for them, but they can't help themselves, so they buy it anyway. The big difference is if they gorge themselves on sugar and glaze and gain eighty pounds, it doesn't ruin *my* life, but their voting for Trump does.

L **is for Liar.** There are at least thirty-four different types of
lies, apparently. I won't list them all here, because I don't
have the time—I'm due at Mount Sinai Hospital in ten minutes
to start my shift as head of Cardiology.

Okay, you caught me. I'm lying—and that would be a lie of
fabrication, i.e., just making shit up. Some of the most common lies are lies of: disinformation, omission, fraud, dissembling, defamation, cover-up, and my favorite, the bald-faced
lie. Why is that my favorite? Because of its etymology. An
eighteenth-century British term, it was originally *bare-faced
lie*, because it was believed that men without beards were more
transparent. It eventually morphed into *bald-faced lie*, and
then into *Boldfaced lie*, which is when a man has no beard but
has covered his face with laundry detergent. (Okay, that's silly,
but so what—who cares?)

There are a few types of people who routinely lie, especially
children and politicians.

Young children don't usually lie very effectively, as lying
is an acquired skill. For better or worse, little kids are pain-
fully honest. If you ask a six-year-old, "Isn't Aunt Immaculata
pretty?" and she's not, he'll say, "No, she's ugly."

(FYI: not all six-year-olds would be so crass. I'm bragging
here, but my grandson is far too brilliant to say something
like that. If I asked him, "Isn't Aunt Immaculata pretty?" he'd
say, "Not particularly, Nana. She has heavy-lidded eyes, a pro-
truding brow, and a weak chin. To say nothing of her upper
lip, which is in desperate need of a cream depilatory. And don't
forget her provolone legs.")

As children get older, they learn to lie to protect themselves from getting caught doing something wrong. For example, my neighbors Paul and Amy Nussbaum have a nine-year-old daughter named, let's call her Bella. (They named her Bella because they think she's beautiful. Don't ask my grandson if *he* thinks she's beautiful.) I stopped over there one night to watch *Celebrity Jeopardy*. (I love that they dumb down the questions for the stars, so they don't look like idiots.) Right before they started Final Jeopardy—the category was "Celebrities Appearing on *Jeopardy* Tonight"—Bella came out of the kitchen with pistachio ice cream all over her face. Amy said, "Did you eat the ice cream I told you not to eat?" Bella looked her right in the eye and said, "No, the cat ate it." It was clear Bella was lying, not because of the evidence all over her face, but because the Nussbaums don't have a cat.

By now, Bella has probably grown out of making stuff up because, for most children, lying is a phase, and with time, maturity, and proper parenting (assuming the parents aren't the Madoffs), most children outgrow it.

Not so much with politicians. All politicians bend the truth, tell people what they want to hear, and offer promises they know they can't fulfill.

During the 1928 presidential campaign, Herbert Hoover promised "a chicken in every pot and a car in every garage." How did he see that happening? For starters, in 1928 the U.S. population was 120,500,000 people. Assuming an average of two people per household, where was Hoover going to find 60 million chickens? On a Mormon chicken farm? And how did he plan to deliver them to every home, pink and fresh and ready for eatin'? A flying coop the size of Noah's Ark? And as for a car in every garage, I grew up in Brooklyn; we lived in a tenement building. What was Hoover going to do, park a Buick on the stoop? While technically Hoover was lying, I'm assuming he said the chicken-pot-car-garage thing as a metaphor for American prosperity, not as an actual promise he couldn't keep.

In 1992, George Bush Sr. famously said, "Read my lips, no new taxes," and then raised taxes. That lie famously cost him the election.

In 1997, Bill Clinton said, "I did not have sex with that woman," which, of course, was a lie. What he should have said was, "I did not provide dry-cleaning services for that woman."

Perhaps the most famous (infamous?) lie of all came in 2003, when George W. Bush started the war in Iraq because "there were weapons of mass destruction" there. There weren't; it was a lie. (Unless, of course, he believed it and, fifteen years later, he's still

is for **Liar**. In 1997, Bill Clinton said, "I did not have sex with that woman," which, of course, was a lie. What he should have said was, "I did not provide dry-cleaning services for that woman."

looking for them, in much the same way O.J. is still looking for Nicole's real killer).

Those political lies stand out because they were aberrations, not the norm. Donald Trump lies so often and so frequently that the *truth* stands out—or at least it will, if he ever tells it.

Donald Trump tells all kinds of lies. He tells lies of defamation (that Ted Cruz's father was involved in the JFK assassination, for example); lies of dissembling, which is lying by posing as someone you're not (Trump used to call journalists and pretend he was his own publicist); lies of deception (he fired Comey because of the "way he handled the Hillary email investigation"; even *Trump* didn't believe that one!); lies of fabrication (he said Muslims in New Jersey were cheering on 9/11); and my favorite, bald-faced lies (for example, about the size of the crowd at his inauguration, in spite of aerial photos proving that what he was saying was patently false).

The truly fascinating thing is that Trump lies when it's unnecessary and for no apparent reason. To this day, he carries on about how he was at the top of his class at Wharton Business School, a lie that (a) is not true, (b) was about something from fifty years ago, and (c) *nobody* cares about. If I said I was the Queen of Sweden from 1963 to 1964, it would clearly be a lie, but would you give a flying fuck? No. You'd just wonder why I would lie about something like that.

Which brings us to the real problem with Trump's lying: credibility. If he's lying about inconsequential things, how will we know if he's telling the truth about big things, like a nuclear attack or a health pandemic or whether he's hung like a horse, as he claims? It's hard to trust someone who lies constantly. The philosopher Friedrich Nietzsche said it best: "I'm not upset that you lied to me, I'm upset that from now on I can't believe you." (He was deep.)

Donald Trump is like an adult version of the character in Aesop's fable "The Boy Who Cried Wolf." The boy lied and lied and lied about the wolf coming for his sheep, and then, one day, the wolf really did come, but nobody helped the boy fight the wolf off because they no longer believed him. In the end, the boy was eaten by the wolf. I think that if Trump keeps on compulsively lying, sooner or later no one will believe him, and he'll get eaten by the wolf. And so will we, even though we have not been the ones doing all the lying. And that pisses me off.

M **is for Alicia Machado.** Alicia Machado was 1996's Miss Universe, the one Trump called "Miss Piggy" because she gained a few pounds after winning the title. He also called her "Miss Housekeeping," because she was from South America. (She was Miss Venezuela.) This all came to light during the campaign, when Hillary Clinton mentioned Alicia and the degrading things Trump had said about her.

I wouldn't be surprised if, when Trump is in the Situation Room (the one in the White House, not the one with Wolf Blitzer) with his national security team—ignoring all the generals as they try to give him strategic intel on urgent issues involving Iran and ISIS—he's thinkng about Alicia Machado and how she should be contacting Jenny Craig.

M **is for Mainstream Media.** *Mainstream media* is the term Republicans use to denigrate any news outlet other than Fox, Brietbart, or Infowars—in other words, any actual, real news outlet. When people say, "I don't know what publications to believe anymore," I tell them, "Breitbart was established in 2005 and Infowars started in 2004, which was when the Internet and fake news were coming into their own. Compare that to the *New York Times*, which started publishing in 1851, and the *Washington Post*, in 1877." If those two publications had been giving us "alternative facts" all that time, I doubt that they would still be in business. Whom are you gonna believe: Woodward and Bernstein, or Conway and Bannon? I rest my case.

M **is for Mar-a-Lago.** Mar-a-Lago is Donald Trump's vacation mansion in Palm Beach, Florida. If you're not familiar with Palm Beach, it's where rich, old, white people go to get some sun and eat watercress sandwiches. And if you're not familiar with Mar-a-Lago, it's the Playboy Mansion with six fewer germs in the hot tub. For years, Donald Trump has been going to Mar-a-Lago every weekend, to relax, play golf, and buy and/or con other rich people. And up until January 21, 2017, he paid for those weekends himself. Now we, the taxpayers, pay for them—because why spend money feeding poor people or helping sick children when we can use that money to make sure that a handful of foreign billionaires have clean towels and fresh fruit on the lanai?

Mar-a-Lago was originally built by socialite and billionaire Post cereal heiress Marjorie Merriweather Post. She envisioned it as a winter retreat for American presidents, and after she died in 1973—she was buried in a beautiful bowl of Grape-Nuts and strawberries—MMP willed the estate to the nation. Seven years later, the nation gave it back, saying, "What, are you crazy? This place costs a fortune to run." In stepped Donald Trump, who made a ridiculously lowball offer for the property, which the Post family turned down. But rather than letting go and moving on with his life, Trump decided to be a petty, vindictive, small-minded prick (and by that, I mean "himself") and bought a strip of land between Mar-a-Lago and the beach. He threatened to build a high-rise that would block Mar-a-Lago's view of the ocean, and thus lower its value. Needless to say, he bullied his way into getting Mar-a-Lago on the cheap. He would call that a good deal; most people would call it extortion. And finally, in 2017, Marjorie Merriweather Post's dream of having Mar-a-Lago serve as a winter White House has come true—as has Donald Trump's dream of having other people pay for it.

M **is for Marco Rubio.** During the 2016 campaign, Candidate Trump kept insulting Rubio by calling him "Little Marco." Was that because he was short? So what? Paul Simon is short (he writes great songs), Tom Cruise is short (which allows him to jump up onto couches easily), and Danny DeVito is really short (but funny and adorable). So, was "little" actually a reference to a certain body part? (Remember, Trump bragged about not having "any problem in that area, believe me." Okay, we believe you. Feel better? Again, so what? Gary Cooper was known to be well endowed—just ask Patricia Neal—and he was a pretty good actor, but could he run a country? Probably not.) Either way, the intent was to diminish Rubio in the eyes of the electorate. So, what can we learn from this? When it comes to being president of the United States, it's better that the country be well run than that the president be well hung.

Republicans *love* Marco Rubio. They think he's perfect for the future of the party—very conservative, very religious, under ninety years old, and hetero. I think he's perfect for them, too, but for different reasons: he's terrible with money, and he lies. Rubio used GOP credit cards for personal use, had a home facing foreclosure, had to liquidate a retirement account, and put family members on his payroll. He also lied about when his parents came to America. Over the years, Rubio told everyone a heartfelt story about how his parents fled Cuba in 1959, when dictator Fidel Castro took over. The truth is, they came to America in 1956, three years *before* the revolution. And contrary to what Marco says, they flew to Miami on a plane; they didn't swim here disguised as porpoises.

M **is for Marriage(s)**. Donald Trump has been involved in 3,500 lawsuits (3,502 if you throw in his divorces). Whatever. Who's judging? The point is, when The Donald says, "I do," he *doesn't*. Maybe he just should replace "I do" with "perhaps" or "maybe" or "I'll get back to you."

Marriage is the last thing (okay, one of *many* last things) Donald Trump should be allowed to weigh in on, yet, as president, he can and does. Same-sex marriage is still a hot-button issue for Republicans. Some of them can't fathom two men or two women falling in love; some of them are buttinsky religious zealots; and some of them just don't want neighbors who have better taste than they do.

M is for **Melania,** the first First Lady who is actually the president's third lady.

Trump has flip-flopped on the issue of same-sex marriage regularly. While he's never been pro-same-sex marriage, in a

2000 interview in *The Advocate*, he said marriage equality was an issue for the states. (If you're not familiar with *The Advocate*, ask your husband's boyfriend what it is.) More recently, in a November 2013 interview on *60 Minutes* with Lesley Stahl, he said the matter of marriage equality had already been "settled" by the Supreme Court. Yet, shortly after taking office, he overturned a transgender rights bill and said he would appoint very conservative Supreme Court justices—his first turned out to be Neil Gorsuch—who would likely overturn the same-sex marriage laws if a case came before the court. I don't know what Trump actually believes, but then, no one does. He's like the offspring of the Sphinx and the Riddler. But standing *right behind him* is the Anti-gay Whisperer, Mike "the Top" Pence. This guy wants to use conversion therapy to turn gays straight. (Interestingly, no one ever wants to use conversion therapy to turn straights gay. Why is that?)

M is for Mars. Donald Trump has ordered NASA to go to Mars in his first term, even though he originally signed a bill directing that it get there by the 2030s. What's his hurry? Is he afraid that fellow billionaire Elon "Big Fingers" Musk or Richard "Huge Hands" Branson will beat him to the punch and get there first? Does Trump know something we don't know? I'm kidding. What are the odds of that?

But Trump *could* have some secret information—like how he's planning to destroy the earth and build a bunch of gaudy Mars-a-Lago on the Red Planet. Or he wants to open a couple of mines and bring coal back from Mars (after which he can take credit as a "job creator" and blame Obama for the high unemployment rates on other planets). But because his record so far on climate change has been horrendous, I'm guessing he's planning a getaway before Mar-a-Lago turns into Chernobyl.

Maybe Trump wants to go to Mars to host some brand-new reality shows up there, like *Dancing with the Aliens* or *Mars's Top Chef* or *Martian Apprentice*. He could sit there and vote people off the galaxy. Talk about an ego trip.

The whole Martian thing is tedious. I couldn't even sit through the Matt Damon movie. But I'll tell you something, if Trump ever gets a second term (God forbid), I'm on the next spaceship outta here!

M **is for Masturbation.** In 2007, Ted Cruz was working for the Texas attorney general, Greg Abbott, who is now that state's governor. On Abbott's behalf, Cruz filed a brief with the U.S. Court of Appeals, requesting a ban on "dildos, vibrators, and other obscene devices." Cruz said that Americans have no right to masturbate. The Dutch, *ja*. The French, *oui*. The Italians, *sicuro*. But Americans, *nyet*. Cruz actually said, "There is no substantive due-process right to stimulate one's genitals for non-medical purposes unrelated to procreation or outside of an interpersonal relationship." Needless to say, Cruz lost the lawsuit. Thank God, otherwise no more sitting on the washing machine for my aunt Immaculata. (FYI: in those days Cruz was known not as "Lyin' Ted," but "Blue Balls Cruz.")

Ironically, Ted Cruz is one of the biggest dildos out there.

M **is for Media**. President Bannon—I mean White House "advisor" Bannon—has declared the media to be "the enemy of the people." Ironic, in that the guy sitting in the Oval Office got there only because of his ability to manipulate and use the media for his personal gain. Donald Trump doesn't hate the media. In fact, in a weird way, he loves them. (Not as weird as the way he loves his daughter, but weird nonetheless.)

Trump loves the media because, without them, he's nothing. Take away the TV coverage, newspaper headlines, and magazine covers, and he's just another invisible rich guy who made a career off his daddy's money—kind of like Hans and Fritz are doing now. What Trump wants is for his *base* to hate the media.

The media are the friends of the people. If it weren't for the media, Nixon might still be in the White House (he'd be dead, but he'd be there), the Vietnam War might still be going on, and the Kardashians would just be Armenian American girls with generous derrieres and thick eyebrows.

M **is for Melania**. Melania Trump is not only beautiful, but she is also a lot of "firsts." She is the First Lady. She is the first First Lady from Slovenia. She is the first First Lady who has a jewelry line. She is the first First Lady who is actually the president's *third* lady. And she is the first First Lady to tell her husband, "Do whatever the fuck you want" in five different languages.

M is for **Meryl Streep.** When Meryl Streep made an impassioned anti-Trump political speech at the 2017 Golden Globes (though she never mentioned his name), the president-elect did what any president-elect would do: he made nasty, petty, childish remarks about her on Twitter. At least, that's what any president-elect of a middle school class would do. Any other president-elect *of the United States* would have done something entirely different—most likely nothing. But no, the Tangerine Tornado took his phone out of his Miley Cyrus backpack and tweeted, "Meryl Streep, one of the most over-rated actresses in Hollywood, doesn't know me but attacked me last night at the Golden Globes. She is a Hillary flunky who lost big."

Meryl Streep is a lot of things, but overrated isn't one of them. She has won 156 awards for her work in film, television, and music. In 2011, she received a Kennedy Center Honor, and in 2014 she was awarded the Presidential Medal of Freedom. I also hear she'll be up for Most Valuable Player in the National Hockey League in 2018. But Meryl's got these serious character flaws: she hates bullies, she tells the truth, and she speaks her mind. The Tweeting Tyrant can't tolerate such horrific attributes. Knowing Meryl as well as I do—every other Wednesday, Mer and I go to the local Y, swim a couple of laps, shoot some hoops, and wax our legs—Trump's tweets didn't bother her at all. Not because they were petulant and inane, but because they weren't really personal. Sure, they were about her, but he sends out nasty tweets about anybody who hurts his feelings. I think all those UV rays from the tanning booth have penetrated his thin skin. There are other high-achieving famous people whom Donald Trump may have called overrated:

- **Noah:** Over-rated. No taste. He thinks THAT'S a boat? Ha. No casino, no lounge. No wonder only animals would book this "cruise."
- **Sir Edmund Hillary**: Climb a mountain on foot? No way. I'd take my private helicopter to top of Everest. I have money. Climbing over-rated. #Sad!
- **Nelson Mandela:** A black John McCain. He got JAILED. I like people who don't get jailed. #BlackLivesOver-rated.
- **Winston Churchill:** Bigly over-rated. Would've lost wars if not for Patton. Fatties can't lead a charge.
- **Gandhi:** Skinny loser. Wears white after Labor Day. But not at Mar-a-Lago. He'll never be invited.
- **The Pope:** Stole my first name, THE. I've been THE Donald way longer than he's been THE Pope. And Francis is a girl's name. #nicedress
- **Albert Einstein:** Genius? I don't think so. Didn't speak English good. I have better brain #JewsNotThatSmartExceptJared #over-rated

M **is for Miranda Warning.** I watch a lot of crime and police procedural shows on Discovery ID. I first got hooked in the '90s, watching *NYPD Blue*. Remember Dennis Franz's tush? I sure do. Hot. Anyway, one of the most important rights we have as citizens is that if we get arrested, the police have to read us our Miranda rights: "You have the right to remain silent, you have the right to counsel . . ." But in 2016, the Supreme Court weakened the Miranda rights, making it okay for police to use evidence obtained in an illegal search, and it created loopholes for police to get into your house without a formal warrant, among other things. I know, I know—you're thinking, *But, Joy, if you didn't do anything wrong, why would you care about the police coming into your house?* My answer is: Because what if I haven't vacuumed, or there are dishes in the sink, or my Spanx are hanging over the shower curtain rod to dry (or, worse, I'm wearing Spanx and nothing else)? That's why. No one should see that. We need to keep the Miranda warning in place. If they want to change it, how about they change it just for Donald Trump? Every morning, a police officer goes into the Oval Office and tells him, "We have a right for *you* to remain silent." I just pray they don't take away the Carmen Miranda warning: "You have the right to wear bananas on your head no matter how crazy everyone thinks you are."

M is for *Mishpocha*. *Mishpocha* is Yiddish. It means "extended family." So, when my three hundred Catholic relatives came to our house for Easter dinner, my mother would say, "Joy, make sure we have enough linguini. The whole *mishpocha* is coming over." (Although my mother was Catholic, she would hook on to an apt Yiddish word when she heard it.) We've never seen Donald with his whole *mishpocha*. We've seen parts of his *mishpocha*. We've seen him with his wives, Ivana, Marla, and Melania. We've seen him with his kids (especially the two and a half he likes), and we've even seen him with Mr. Ivanka, Jared Kushner. Yet, we've hardly ever seen Hans's and Fritz's wives. I know both sons are married; I've seen wedding bands on their fingers in those photos where they're holding up the dead animals they've gunned down. So, what's the story? Are the wives Mexican? Are they Muslim? Are they men? Or, most important, are they still under warranty? I'm joking, of course. Truth be told, Hans and Fritz's wives fit the Trump mold precisely: they're blonde amazons who look like they could step on you at Neiman Marcus and never even notice it.

M **is for Miss Universe Pageant**. Putting the predator in chief in charge of a beauty pageant is like putting George W. Bush in charge of an English class—nothing good is going to come out of it. Trump brags about sexually assaulting women; he shouldn't even be allowed to attend a beauty pageant, let alone own one.

In 2011, I was a judge for the Miss America Pageant. It was a lot of fun. The women were smart and thoughtful and beautiful. And I can tell you for a fact—a real fact, not an alternative one—that there's no way the people who ran Miss America would insult or disparage any of the contestants. Yet, that's what The Donald routinely did to the contestants in *his* pageants—that is, when he wasn't wandering into their dressing rooms unannounced. And he didn't even need to do that; he could have had the microwaves spy on them.

M is for Mistake. George W. Bush once famously (infamously?) said he couldn't recall making any mistakes. I guess saying mission accomplished, blowing up the deficit, destroying the economy, and creating a housing crisis slipped his mind. Donald Trump is the same—he never apologizes for anything because he doesn't think he makes mistakes. There is a clinical psychological term for a person who believes he never makes mistakes: *liar*.

M is for Moron. Donald Trump and his Merry Band of Misfits don't seem to know much. In fact, they might be morons— which is something of a backhanded compliment, because there is an actual medical scale of stupidity, and "moron" is *not* at the bottom. The scale is based on standardized IQ testing. There are specific terms to describe various levels of intelligence. For example, an imbecile is smarter than an idiot. And a moron is smarter than an imbecile. So, Donald, when it comes to the stupid scale, be proud! You're a moron! Don't ever, ever, ever let anyone call you an idiot! That word is saved for Rick Perry. And Dan Quayle. And Michelle Bachmann. And that crazy ex-governor Annie Oakley from Alaska.

M is for Mr. Magoo. When I was a little girl, *Mr. Magoo* was one of my favorite Saturday morning cartoons. Magoo was a little old man who wore glasses with triple-thick Coke bottle lenses but was basically blind. Every week, he would drive all over town, almost crashing his car or driving off a cliff. Even though he couldn't see anything, he always came away unscathed. Everyone around him, however, was scared to death and in constant peril, yet Magoo kept right on driving, knocking things over everywhere he went. Now, with Trump, I think life is imitating art—if you replace the glasses with bad hair and tiny hands.

M **is for Mussolini.** It's become very trendy to compare Donald Trump to Benito Mussolini. They have a similar scowl, neither one is ever seen laughing, neither speaks English, and both walk like they're carrying a Genoa salami in their pants. There is one big difference, however. Mussolini made the trains run on time. Trump shredded the Amtrak budget so the trains may not run at all.

N is for Nancy Reagan. When Nancy Reagan started out as First Lady, she was not very popular. People saw her as a cold, calculating, entitled Hollywood diva. (Kind of the same way Republicans see me, except that I live in New York and I don't gaze at my husband like a dog looking at a pork chop. More on that in a minute.) At the same time that President Reagan was declaring, "Let them eat ketchup (as a vegetable)," Nancy was playing Marie Antoinette of Washington, spending a fortune on new china for the White House. She had two sets of dishes at all times, which begs the question: was Nancy Reagan kosher? She also used to give Ronnie policy advice, but only after she'd consulted astrologists instead of experts. How crazy was that? I don't want our national security based on someone's moon being in retrograde. I want it based on someone's ass being in a library.

But then John Hinckley Jr. shot Reagan because he wanted to impress Jodie Foster so she'd go out with him—that's delusional on so many levels—and public opinion toward Nancy began to change. And when Reagan developed Alzheimer's disease, people's opinion of Nancy softened even more. I felt bad for her; I wouldn't wish that on anyone, but I also know that she didn't go up against Republican dogma and speak out in favor of stem cell research until *after* it affected her personally. But at least she finally did get it. Unlike Mitch McConnell, who had polio as a child and was treated at Warm Springs, for free, but now wants to cut medical benefits for the indigent. Some people never learn. Let's just say he's an ingrate with a short memory.

And as for the gazing thing—I've never gotten over that. Nancy would look at Ronnie with this creepy, glazed stare, like she'd just gotten off the bus from Stepford. Look, I love my husband, but if I ever sit there and stare at him for hours on end without blinking or moving, it won't be because I'm wildly in love, but because I'm dead.

N is for Neo-Nazis. Not to be confused with the old, original Nazis. No, these are new and improved Nazis! The old Nazis were subtler than the new ones. For starters, the neo-Nazis have lots and lots of tattoos; the old Nazis rarely had tattoos, and if they had, they would have been small, maybe a petite I ♥ ADOLF on one ankle. The neos have tattoos all over the place: on their hands, their heads, their necks, their faces. If you see a guy with a swastika on his lips, you're not going to have to think, *Geez, I wonder what that's about?* Old Nazis, though, would discreetly try to find out if you were in their corner. A Nazi official would walk up to a woman on the street and say, "Hello, Fraulein, what are your plans for . . . Chanukah?" And she'd say, "What's a Chanukah?" and then they'd both laugh and laugh and march down the street to an Oktoberfest party, even though it was only April.

The Trump administration only semi-tries to distance itself from the alt-right neo-Nazis. And I say "semi-try" because they never really come out and say, "We don't want your crazy-ass, hateful, racist, anti-Semitic votes," because they *do* want those votes. Team Trump needs that part of the base to come out and vote, so they say just enough to appear not okay with neo-Nazis to appease their nonracist constituents, but not enough to alienate the neo-Nazis themselves.

My question is: Why are the hate groups and neo-Nazis drawn to the Republican Party? Do they prefer elephants over donkeys? Do they look better in red than blue? You don't see an army of skinheads and neo-Nazis at Democratic Party events, do you? Why is that, I wonder?

N is for Nepotism. It's not unusual for presidents to have trusted family members give them advice in the West Wing. Bill Clinton put Hillary in charge of health care, and George W. Bush used to call on Jeb all the time, primarily to ask him how to pronounce the big words. And of course, JFK appointed his brother Robert to be attorney general, which caused Congress to write the anti-nepotism law in 1967 in reaction.

There is some debate over whether the law applies as high up as the White House. This has prompted Trump to appoint his son-in-law, Jared Kushner, to be a senior advisor. He also named his daughter Ivanka "special assistant to the president," without a salary, to skirt the law. (No matter—it's been reported that the Kushners are worth 740 million buckaroos, in any case.) Ivanka will have an office in the White House near the Oval Office, so that Daddy can check her out when she's not looking. They're waiting for Barron to hit puberty so they can make him secretary of energy. In that case, I don't mind. The kid is probably smarter than Rick ("Oops") Perry.

N is for New Mexico. The country Trump plans to wall off as soon as he builds his big, beautiful wall across Old Mexico. And he's going to make New Mexico pay for it.

N is for Newt Gingrich. Has there ever been a sleazier human being? I think not. Oh, sure, he's mean-spirited and hypocritical, but like they say on infomercials, "Wait, there's more!" Newt has also been married three times, and served his second wife with divorce papers while she was being treated for cancer. At least he eventually acknowledged that he was cheating with a congressional aide during the time he was leading the impeachment proceedings against President Clinton. Enough said.

N is for Nikki Haley. The former governor of South Carolina was named the U.S. ambassador to the United Nations. Compared to other Republicans, she's a breath of the fresh air we're running out of—meaning, she's relatively bright and appears to be sane. Unless the Republicans skew even farther to the right—in which case, they'll fall off the end of the earth (you know at least a handful of them still believe the earth is flat)—she may be the future of the Republican Party. Her parents were immigrants from India, and even though she's tough on illegal immigration, she doesn't want to build a wall across the Atlantic and Indian Oceans. She was against the anti-transgender bathroom bill, which is good for the LGBTQ community. On the downside, she's rabidly antiabortion, which is not good for women. But she also has more balls than the Republican men in Congress in that she stood up to Donald Trump. She said that Trump should release his taxes and that his ban on Muslims was "un-American and un-Constitutional." And when the child in chief began tweeting nasty things about her, she sweetly and condescendingly replied, "Bless his heart." But I'll bet, under her breath, she was mumbling, "What an asshole."

N is for Richard Nixon. I never saw anyone sweat like Richard Nixon did, and I've been line-dancing with Louie Anderson. Every State of the Union speech, there Nixon was, behind the desk, sweating like a pack animal carrying a load across the Andes. For three years, I thought the Oval Office was located in a sauna. Nixon could schvitz in an igloo in January. Check out the Kennedy-Nixon debates—you won't believe your eyes. There was Kennedy, happy, smiling, handsome, looking like he didn't have a care in the world. And there was Nixon, sweating so much it looked like he'd swum to the studio. The most irritating thing is that Nixon had these beads of sweat on his upper lip. I wanted to grab a Kleenex and put my hand through the TV screen and wipe him off. Why was he sweating so much? Was it because he knew he was a liar and a crook?

We can't call Nixon a sociopath; at least he had a clue about himself. I've never seen Trump sweat—seems like lying comes so easily to him it's almost like breathing. That ad that says,

"Never let them see you sweat"? Wrong. When they see you sweat, they know that you know you're a liar.

N **is for No One Knew.** Shortly after taking office, Trump said, "Nobody knew health care could be so complicated." *Everyone* knew. Only *he* didn't. A few months later, after meeting with Chinese leaders to discuss the North Korean situation, he said, "I realized it's not so easy." Again, *everyone* knew. *He* didn't know.

Look, no one expects the president to know everything, but how he did not even know these things were complex? Did he assume that every president, elected official, and expert for the past fifty years were total idiots and couldn't figure these things out, or that they were all dawdling and doing crossword puzzles when they should have been working?

One would think that over the course of an eighteen-month campaign season, Donald Trump would have learned

N is for **Nukeleheads**. Donald Trump has the password to our nuclear codes, and I wouldn't trust him with the password to my Amazon account.

something about the issues at hand, or at least the complexity of them. But one would be wrong. He seemingly learned nothing. I don't know much about splitting the atom, but I'm betting it's not as easy as making a lasagna. I don't know advanced calculus, but I'm pretty sure it's more complicated than balancing my checkbook. One would assume that even if Trump didn't know that these things were complicated, he'd at least be smart enough to keep his mouth shut about it. Again, one would be wrong. It turns out that there are other things The Donald didn't know were complicated:

- Renewable energy
- Rocket science
- High-tech agriculture
- Rising seawater levels
- Combating infectious diseases
- Talking to Siri and Alexa
- Salting a margarita glass
- Working the remote
- Buckles and snaps
- Putting his pajamas on with the fly in the front

N is for Nukeleheads. I'm scared—Donald Trump has the password to our nuclear codes, and I wouldn't trust him with the password to my Amazon account.

North Korea has been testing missiles with the apparent goal of someday getting them to reach the United States. Trump has reacted to these tests as expected—with bluster, bravado, and a "my missiles are bigger than yours" attitude. Since he didn't want to interrupt his golf game at Mar-a-Lago, he sent the whitest man in America, Mike Pence, to the Demilitarized Zone, the area separating North from South Korea, to deliver a "stern warning." Pence stopped praying long enough to say, "We will defeat any attack." North Korea bad, we good! Tarzan love Jane.

All I could think of was *Not this again*. I spent junior high school hiding under my desk (and I didn't even want to be a White House intern). I remember how scared I was during the Cuban Missile Crisis, waiting for Castro to drop atomic bombs on Queens College. I kept screaming, "I don't want to die a virgin!" The fact that I was still a virgin in college tells you how assiduously I avoided any incoming missiles, nuclear or otherwise.

Tensions were so high back then that a lot of suburban homes actually had bomb shelters in case of nuclear attack. (Today, those bomb shelters would go for $2,700 a month: "Subterranean studio apartment, lead walls to guarantee quiet, very private. Romantic underground oasis. If you think the mushroom cloud is hot . . .") The Cold War was terrifying, but I always thought we'd get through it. Why would any country start a nuclear war? Surely the leaders knew that they would be vaporized along with the rest of us. When JFK was president, I assumed he knew what he was doing, and in fact, he did. He made a secret deal with everyone's favorite shoe banger, Nikita Khrushchev, and the missiles pointing directly at Queens College campus went away.

Which brings me to the present.

Khrushchev and Kennedy have been replaced by Kim Jong-un and Donald Trump. Smart albeit tough political adversaries have been replaced by a couple of guys out on a day pass from Crazytown. Kim Jong-un, the leader of North Korea, is a total whack job. Everyone in the world agrees he's irrational, unpredictable, and belongs in a looney bin—if for no other reason than the hair and the outfits. No sane person who looks in the mirror and sees *that* staring back at him says, "Love it. I'm good to go." We, in turn, have Donald Trump, who's not as whacko as the Korean cracko, but he's on the A-Team of Ignorance. Do we trust Trump to get us through this in one piece? I'm afraid he might bomb North Dakota by accident. Does Trump even know who Kim Jong-un is? He seemed to get him mixed up with his father, Kim Jong-il, who's been dead for six years. It's entirely possible Trump thinks General Tso is the president of China and that the Queen of England is a cross-dressing dancer called Dave.

I can't go through the nuclear nonsense again. I don't want

to be afraid, and I have no interest in hiding under my desk, praying that those in charge know what's happening (my teachers sure didn't) and will fix things. The only good thing about being sent back to Queens College is that I'd be a virgin again. At least it would give me something to look forward to.

O is for Ohio. As John King and Steve Kornacki and Wolf Blitzer and every other newshound "manning the map" on Election Night tell us over and over and over again, "No Republican has ever won the White House without winning Ohio," and, "As Ohio goes, so goes the country." Does this mean I have to be mad at Ohio for the next four years? I hope not. I like Ohio. Some of my favorite people are from Ohio: Erma Bombeck, Gloria Steinem, Dean Martin. Clark Gable was from Cadiz, Ohio (his ears were from Wisconsin); astronauts Neil Armstrong and John Glenn were from Ohio; as were writers Zane Grey, Toni Morrison, and James Thurber. Steven Spielberg is from Cincinnati, Rob Lowe was raised in Dayton, and Paul Newman was from Cleveland. What I'm saying is that I can't hold a grudge against Ohio. Yes, they fucked up in 2016 by voting for Con Man the Vulgarian, but they also reelected the Democratic senator Sherrod Brown, so I'll look away and call it a draw. But if they do it again, in 2020, I'll never set foot in Ohio again, not even to go to the Rock and Roll Hall of Fame—unless I'm voted in.

O is for Opioid Crisis. I love saying "Big Pharma"; it reminds me of a lesbian Phys Ed major from Bangladesh I knew in college.

O is for Oil. If you want to know how Trump got to the White House, think about the Watergate story and "follow the money." What business are the Koch brothers in? The oil business. What does the Dakota Access Pipeline bring from Canada? Oil. Who will make money off the Dakota Access Pipeline? The Koch brothers. Who will make money having Trump in the White House? The Koch brothers. Whom should we never see nude oil wrestling? The Koch brothers. Truth be told, the only oil I'm interested in is Oil of Olay. Because if Trump does bring us to the point of Armageddon, why not go out with nice, silky smooth skin?

O is for O.J. Simpson. If you're thinking, *Joy's connecting Trump and O.J. because one was nicknamed the Juice and the other is the color of juice*, you'd be wrong. Apparently, the two were friends. O.J. was at Donald's wedding to Marla Maples, along with Don King, Rosie O'Donnell, and me. I don't know what I'm more creeped out about—that I met O.J., or that I was at one of Trump's weddings. All I know is there wasn't a wet eye in the house.

O is for Olfactory Senses. Or, Trump sniffing. During the presidential debates, Donald Trump kept sniffing and making these creepy snorting sounds. At first, I thought he was doing cocaine, but then I remembered that he didn't even drink, so that couldn't have been it. Then I thought maybe he had allergies—maybe he was allergic to Hillary's pantsuits or, more likely, her impressive résumé, but that didn't seem likely. (He's spent his whole life being around people much smarter than he, and this sniffing thing is new.) And then I thought maybe one of those violent Mexican thugs he talks about snuck over the border and used a shiv to punch a hole in his septum while he slept. But that, too, seemed far-fetched. Finally, though, after much contemplation (i.e., two glasses of white wine), I realized that Trump simply had heightened olfactory senses, and he wasn't so much sniffing as smelling. And after even more contemplation (I switched from white to red), I realized that what he was smelling that was so foul it made him sniff and snort was the bullshit coming out of his own mouth.

O is for Opioid Crisis. It was a shock for me to learn that the largest opioid consumption in America is going on in the Red states. That's right, the states that voted overwhelmingly for Donald John Trump. This means that in addition to Russia interfering to help Trump win, and FBI director James Comey perfectly timing his scathing, yet frivolous announcement that the Bureau was reopening its investigation into Hillary Clinton's emails, it looks like a lot of the people who pulled the lever for DT could have been high on drugs on Election Day.

In the 1960s, bored housewives began going to their local Dr. Feelgood to get "diet pills" that would help get them through their days. Fifty years later, the diet pills have been replaced by opioids (heroin, the Oxy twins, etc.), and instead of getting people through their days, they're getting them through rehab. There are a few schools of thought as to why we're in an opioid crisis, but one is that depression and a bleak outlook have led people to escape through drugs. How does it help these people to have Trump keep saying how bleak the situation is, that there's carnage everywhere? Americans need to feel uplifted; we don't need Debbie Downer telling us that the country is on the brink of annihilation (especially when it's not true).

A second possible reason for the opioid crisis is that a deregulated pharmaceutical industry has run rampant selling prescription meds. No more need to buy illegal drugs in a back alley from Shaky or Johnny B. Now you can buy them legally from the pharmacist at CVS (usually a guy named Ned who wears a blue smock with a name tag and a pocket protector).

Big Pharma—I love saying, "Big Pharma"; it reminds me of a lesbian Phys Ed major from Bangladesh I knew in college—keeps running ads for drugs that treat diseases I didn't know existed and conditions I didn't know I had. Last night, I was watching *Hoarders*—I love that show; it makes me feel better about my own housekeeping—and at the dramatic turn in the episode ("How was I supposed to know Mama had three dead cats, a compost heap, and a '67 Buick LeSabre in the bathroom?"), they naturally went to a commercial break. And what I got were back-to-back sixty-second ads asking me if I had restless legs or a dry vagina. Well, I don't have restless legs or a dry vagina. I have dry legs and a restless vagina. Do they have drugs for that?

O is for Oprah. There has been talk of Oprah Winfrey running for president. That would be great; she'd win in a landslide. Everyone would vote for her. She checks every box: She's a woman. She's a celebrity. She has a man. She might have a woman. She has an Oscar. She has a network. She has a book club. And most important, she has a weight problem. What's not to like? Oh, and she's rich. Even Trump might vote for her.

O is for Orange. In 2011, Melania Trump was a guest on my show on HLN. As we know, she's beautiful and, even more important, she has style. Her hair and makeup are perfect—not a split end or a splotch in sight. Which makes me wonder: how can she be married to a man who looks like he passed out in a bag of Doritos? Does she not notice that his face is as orange as the Great Pumpkin from the Charlie Brown Halloween special? Or maybe when she hears his voice first thing in the morning, she goes into such a panic that she suffers from hysterical blindness and all she can see coming toward her are those dinosaur arms and tiny hands. He needs a makeover. Maybe Tiffany can start a national Take Your Father Shopping Day, and she can drag him to her favorite makeup counter at Bloomingdale's. Even better, she should take him to Nordstrom, just to piss off Ivanka. Talk about a win-win. Or maybe Hans or Fritz could mention in passing that Dada needs to stop buying his makeup at Sherwin-Williams. Glossy latex enamel is for suburban houses, not human skin. His face clashes with itself.

But worse than the color is the premise: Why does Donald Trump even wear makeup? He's not on *The Apprentice* anymore, so that can't be the reason. In fact, since he took office, he almost never appears in public, and when he does, everyone holds their breath, praying he hasn't started World War

III. The straight men I know wear makeup only if they're on television or onstage. I have a gay friend who wears makeup only to provide contour, because he lives with the delusion that if he appears two pounds thinner, George Clooney will leave Amal and go out with him. (I can relate.)

So, the man and his makeup—yet one more unexplained thing about our president . . . along with his IQ; his tax returns; his mental diagnosis; his foreign, domestic, *and* economic policies; and his "fondness" for Vlad the Impaler.

O is for Overtime. Overtime is what employers should pay their workers if they work more hours than they're required to. Donald Trump and his minions disagree. When Donald drained the swamp, he took the bottom-feeders he found and put them in his Cabinet and his inner circle. Now those soulless, bloodthirsty vultures—oh, I'm sorry, I meant "business-friendly corporate executives"—are looking for ways to allow employers not to have to pay overtime to their employees, usually by cutting hours or changing their employment status. Trump is lucky *he* doesn't work at an hourly rate. Considering how much time he spends vacationing at Mar-a-Lago, we'd only have to pay him two bucks a week.

O is for Oxycodone. A strong, highly addictive opioid painkiller, or as Rush Limbaugh thinks of it, lunch.

O is for Oxycontin. A strong, highly addictive opioid painkiller, or as Rush Limbaugh thinks of it, dinner.

P is for Palin. Not just Sarah, but the whole family: Todd and Bristol and Willow and Azalea and Crabgrass and Trig and Tripp and Track and Trick or Treat.

I love Sarah Palin—not as a human being of course, but as a punch line. She's a comedic jackpot, a modern-day version of slipping on a banana peel or drinking from a dribble cup. The humor keeps flowing, like a urinary tract infection. FYI: I think "Tract" will be the name for Bristol's next kid.

Speaking of Bristol, how great was it that, after constantly getting pregnant out of wedlock, she became the spokesperson for abstinence? Bristol has spent so much time in the backseat of pickup trucks, she should have a Confederate bumper sticker tattooed on her ass. Spokesperson for abstinence? If she were any more unqualified for a job, she'd be a member of Trump's Cabinet.

P.S. I think "Truck" will be the name for Tract's twin brother.

P is for Paranoia. Republican politicians like to traffic in fear, creating a sense of paranoia among their faithful (and, if we're not careful, the rest of us). "Obama is coming for your guns"; "The Chinese are taking your jobs," etc. None of it is true. Last time I checked, Sarah Palin still has her Uzi to mow down moose, and I have yet to meet a disgruntled white guy who lost out to a minority for a job delivering egg rolls and wonton soup to my apartment on a bicycle or coming up with an app for my iPad.

Team Trump has convinced his base to be afraid of Mexicans, African Americans, lesbians, gays, transgender people, Muslims, liberals, Jews, intellectuals, brown people, all sorts of foreigners, CNN, MSNBC, the *Washington Post*, and of course the *New York Times*. Truth be told, I'm more afraid of Team Trump than of any of them. Especially Mike Pence; she scares the hell out of me.

P is for Pence. Creepy Veepy has more issues than *Life* magazine's back catalogue. Mike Pence is fooling no one with all the hateful antigay rhetoric. Pence spends more time obsessing about gay sex than all the members of the Village People combined. Pence's anti-LGBTQ record is so bad that when he went to see the Broadway show *Hamilton*, at the end of the play the cast called him out from the stage. Most of the cast members were black and Hispanic, and some were definitely gay. When the show ended, "Aaron Burr" (wearing a lovely muumuu) stepped forward and, in front of the entire audience, asked Pence if the incoming administration would please be fair and tolerant of *all* Americans, not just the ones it liked. It was a stunning moment. I only wish Pence had gone to see *Avenue Q*. It would have been fun to see a hand puppet tell him to go fuck himself.

Pence also says he won't have lunch or dinner alone with a woman other than his wife. (Notice he doesn't say anything about brunch?) I'm not sure if this is out of some misguided, fake-Christian respect for his wife or because he is *sooooo* darned heterosexual he's afraid he wouldn't be able to control himself and he might leap across the booth at the Olive

Garden and grab him a piece-o-puss like his boss man brags about. What if he were having the Never Ending Pasta Bowl and Mother Teresa, exhausted from washing the feet of the poor, walked in and plopped herself down at his table? Would he spit out his linguini and make a handsy lunge at the Saint of Calcutta?

But in spite of (or maybe because of) his flaming homophobia, mainstream Republicans seem to like Pence. I think it's because, compared to Trump, Pence seems reasonable and normal. Of course, compared to Trump, *Mad Money*'s Jim Cramer seems reasonable and normal. Mike Pence presents well; he's like a pit bull at the Westminster Kennel Club Dog Show. When he's being paraded in front of cameras and judges, he looks pretty and acts nice, but the minute he's backstage, he's harassing poodles and humping dachsunds.

And he's the *perfect* VP choice for Trump. Here's why:

- He has normal hair. It's a silver, close-cropped "Welcome to 1953" style. Makes him look like a drill sergeant in the army.

- He provides cover for Trump with the evangelical base. In their heart of hearts, the evangelicals *must* know that Trump is a malevolent, cheating, womanizing heathen. They're much more comfortable with a malevolent, faithful homophobe, as long as he's against abortion.

- He knows how to defend Trump when he lies. For example: In a December 2016 interview, George Stephanopoulos asked

Pence about Trump's penchant for lying. Pence said that Trump's speaking his mind was "refreshing" to the American people. Really? I'm an American people and I don't find it refreshing. The only kind of lying I find refreshing is lying by the pool on a lounge chair with a glass of white wine while Jon Hamm fetches me grapes and gives me a pedicure.

P is for Pets. Nearly every president in modern history has had a First Dog, you know, one that runs around the White House, plays in the Rose Garden, and poops in the Blue Room. The Obamas had Bo, the Bushes had Miss Beazley, the Nixons had Checkers, the Clintons had Bill. Donald Trump is such a narcissist I don't know if he's capable of caring for a dog, but if he is . . . he'd probably get a Chihuahua. Not because they're small or cute, but because when he gets bored, he could just deport it back to the shelter it tunneled out of in search of a job at Taco Bell.

P is for Plagiarism. Or, as Melania calls it, writing. When I watched Melania's speech at the Republican National Convention, I was quite impressed. It was well written, on point, and beautifully delivered—and familiar! DUH. (Truth be told,

is for **Pussy Grabber**. How do you grab a pussy? Easy. Walk up to Paul Ryan, take him by the collar, and say, "Get over here, you, spineless little twit!"

Melania has a better command of the English language than Donald does, which *is* surprising, given that she's from Slovenia and he's from Queens. But I digress.)

The day after her speech, we all discovered that part of it had been lifted directly from Michelle Obama's 2012 speech at the Democratic National Convention. Melania plagiarized a Democrat, meaning they're not just stealing our money; they're also stealing our words.

To be fair, it's not like Melania had written the speech herself—all high-end political figures have speechwriters. But shouldn't they also have fact-checkers? Or at least alternative-fact-checkers, if that's what they're more comfortable with. Instead, they let the poor woman go out and hang herself in front of the whole country. Maybe that's why she has barely left Trump Tower since Shavuos (a Jewish holiday that sounds funny, even though it's not the one where a guy blows the shofar).

P is for Prenup. For the record, I became a believer in prenups when Anna Nicole Smith had to fight for money after her two-hundred-year-old billionaire husband died and his adult children battled her for his fortune. A rock-solid prenup, with special competency clauses in place, would have prevented such ugliness. My own personal feeling is that if Anna Nicole could go down on that withered schlong, she was entitled to every nickel the old goat had.

I know for a fact that Donald Trump always has strong prenups in place, which, given how often he gets married, is a good idea. What I don't know for a fact are the details of the prenups, but given the public statements his ex-wives have made, they must include things like "She'll only say how wonderful I am," "She'll say I'm great in bed," and "I get full custody of the bobby pins and White Rain hair products."

P is for Purell. Donald Trump suffers from mysophobia, an unnatural fear of germs. (Although, he probably doesn't think he suffers from it; he probably thinks *I've got the best phobia. Nobody has phobias as good as mine. I'm a great phobic.*) Trump doesn't like to shake hands with people, but, to be fair, neither does another famous germaphobe, Howie Mandel. Which explains why, when Howie and The Donald met, instead of shaking hands, they engaged in a deep, slow tongue kiss, complete with moaning and tingly feelings in their stomachs. Just kidding—I like Howie and wouldn't wish this on him.

P is for Pussy Grabber. How do you grab a pussy? Easy. Walk up to Paul Ryan, take him by the collar, and say, "Get over here, you, spineless little twit!"

Actually, how *do* you grab a woman by her pussy? Not sure. It's not like the puss sticks out like a penis—or like Rick Perry in a bookstore. Unless a woman is a freak of nature, and has looser lips than Julius and Ethel Rosenberg, the puss is almost impossible to grab onto—then again, if the man has extremely tiny hands . . . (See: *Tiny Hands.*)

Q is for Queens. I don't mean Elizabeth or Beatrix or Latifah. I mean the New York City borough where Donald Trump was born. For those of you not familiar with New York City, it's made up of five boroughs: Manhattan, Brooklyn, Queens, Staten Island, and the Bronx. To give you context: the Bronx is where the Yankees play; Queens is where the Mets play; Brooklyn is where the Dodgers used to play; Staten Island is where no one plays; and Manhattan is where Patti LuPone and Bette Midler play.

When Donald Trump was born in 1946, Queens had a population of approximately 1.9 million people, and it was 83 percent white (especially *his* neighborhood, Jamaica Estates, which is the fancy-schmancy part of Jamaica). As of 2010, Queens had a population of approximately 1.6 million and was 57 percent white. See where I'm going with this? Trump's taken the old "there goes the neighborhood" adage and applied it to the whole country. He's brought his anti-immigrant, anti-minority philosophy from Queens to Washington.

is for **Quickie**. In the past, the word quickie was usually used to describe a short sexual escapade. Now it's used to describe the length of Donald Trump's attention span and, probably, the longest sexual escapade he's ever had.

If you doubt this, don't forget that his and Daddy's real estate companies were sued twice (in 1973 and 1982) for racial discrimination in housing. Both times, the Trumps settled with the plaintiffs, even though they were not forced to admit any wrongdoing. (My question: why pay out millions of dollars if you didn't do anything wrong?) Anyway, Trump tried to prevent his buildings from becoming melting pots, and now he's trying to do the same with our country. I hope he fares about as well now as he did then.

Q **is for Questions**. I have so many questions and so little time, but these are the questions I would like answered *today*:

1. **(To the press)** When Trump lies, how come you never stop him and say, "Hey, that's a lie"?
2. **(To Ivanka)** Are you inviting Steve Bannon over for Rosh Hashanah?
3. **(To Bill O'Reilly)** What's your obsession with killing famous historical figures? And who told you falafel is a lubricant?
4. **(To Reince Priebus)** Is that collagen in your lips or are they swollen from kissing Trump's butt?
5. **(To Sean Spicer)** Are you physically afraid of April Ryan?

Q **is for Quiche.** Remember that book *Real Men Don't Eat Quiche*? It's not true. My husband loves quiche and he's a real man. And to prove it, he eats his quiche with a side of concrete. In my opinion, real men don't insult women, don't make vulgar remarks about their own daughters, don't spend nine hours constructing their hair or wear orange makeup. And now I have to go dig up the driveway; I'm making quiche for lunch.

Q is for Quickie. In the past, the word *quickie* was usually used to describe a short sexual escapade. Now it's used to describe the length of Donald Trump's attention span and, probably, the longest sexual escapade he's ever had.

Q is for QVC. For those of you who were heartbroken when Nordstrom, Bloomingdale's, and Neiman Marcus stopped carrying a lot of Ivanka Trump's clothing, jewelry, and accessories (because they were appalled by the administration's divisive policies and language), cry no more. In fact, perk the fuck up! The Ivanka brand is on the QVC TV network! Now you never have to leave your house. You can get any kind of schmata, handbag, or belt you want. You can buy the earrings, necklaces, and bracelets of your choice. And someday, in the not-too-distant future, you may even be able to buy handcuffs and leg irons that are exact replicas of the ones Ivanka's husband will be wearing in Leavenworth. (Talk about Jared the Jeweler!)

Joy Behar

R is for **Raging Bull**. Robert De Niro is a tough interview. He's not a big talker—he gives mainly monosyllabic answers—but Donald Trump has transformed De Niro into Patrick Henry on steroids. De Niro has said of Trump, "I'd like to punch him in the face, he's blatantly stupid, he's a punk, he's a dog, he's a pig, he's a con, he's a bullshit artist, he's a mutt who doesn't know what he's talking about, he doesn't do his homework, doesn't care, he thinks he's gaming society and doesn't pay his taxes."

This is the longest sentence De Niro has uttered since he was in *Mean Streets* in 1973. As Patrick Henry might have said (if he were alive, like Frederick Douglass), "Give me liberty or I'll break both your legs."

R is for **Random Acts of Helpfulness**. The Honda car company has come up with a new program called Random Acts of Helpfulness. People call in or write to Honda and tell them some personal story, and Honda steps in and helps them. It's kind of like *Extreme Makeover*, only with cars. For example, a mother from Pomona called up and said her son was in music school, but his instrument had broken and they couldn't afford to replace it. And the Honda guy said, "We're here to help. We're going to buy your son a new clarinet." And the mother gets all emotional and cries, and all the listeners think, "Aww, isn't that sweet?" (Of course, you never hear the mother say, "That's awfully nice, but he plays the piano.")

Anyway, I would like a Random Act of Helpfulness from Honda: "Dear Honda, this is Joy from New York. My head hurts and my heart is broken, but unlike Russia and the Koch brothers, I can't afford to buy an election. It would be so great if you could help me out and get me a new fucking president."

R **is for Reaganomics.** When David Stockman was the director of the Office of Management and Budget (OMB) from 1981 to 1985, he was known as the "Father of Reaganomics." (This must have been very confusing to Nancy because, as I mentioned earlier, Ronnie called her "Mommy.") Reaganomics is supply-side economics, or the infamous "trickle-down theory," which basically means if you give the wealthiest people in the country even *more* money, eventually it will trickle down to everyone else. (Stockman also hoped this would curtail the "welfare state." As nasty as that sounds, it's still better than the GOP's current plans to curtail the welfare state: deporting people and starving the poor, elderly, and infirm.) Rumor has it that the first time Tip O'Neill heard about Stockman's economic theory, he laughed so hard he felt something trickling down his leg.

And thirty-seven years later, that may be the only thing that has ever trickled down. The Reagan tax cuts for the rich did not help the middle class. They *did*, however, grow the national debt from $79.0 billion to $2.3 *trillion* by the end of Reagan's first term. And since Reaganomics didn't work for anybody but the wealthy the first time, guess what the Republicans are trying to push again in 2017? If you said, "Same bullshit," you'd be right. And how do they get away with it? See: "B is for Base."

R **is for Regis Philbin.** A lot of the nonracist, non-crazy people who voted for Donald Trump were voting for change. They didn't want another politician in the White House; they wanted an outsider. I can appreciate that they were tired of politics as usual, but considering that the field *is* politics, wouldn't it have been a good idea to hire a person with *some* experience in it, or at least rudimentary knowledge of how government works? When I go for my annual endoscopy, I go to a gastroenterologist, not an outsider, like my dog walker or the neighborhood auto body guy. I want someone who actually knows what he's doing.

is for Republicans. Republicans should stay away from my uterus. Whether I use that space to house a fetus or store a winter coat, it's none of Newt Gingrich's business.

According to the most recent UN Census estimates, the population of the United States stands at 326,111,903. Think about that: 326,111,903 people, and the Republicans couldn't find *one* outsider who wasn't racist, misogynistic, xenophobic, or mentally ill to run for office?

If I want an outsider in the White House, I'd go for Regis Philbin. I love Regis; everybody loves Regis. He'd be perfect. He'll appeal to Republicans because he's an old, straight white guy with no governmental experience. He'll appeal to Democrats because

The Great Gasbag

185

he's smart, thoughtful, and lives in New York. He's always in a good mood—he's even friendly early in the morning!—he's a great listener, and on top of that, he was able to deal with the perkiness of Kelly and Kathie Lee for all those years without losing his temper or his lunch. Do you really think Kim Jong-un is going to rattle his cage? Not only that, but Regis can sing, and he has a great stage act. He won't waste a million dollars a day of taxpayer money schlepping to play golf at Mar-a-Lago. He'll grab an Uber and do a show at the Westbury Music Fair. A hundred and eight bucks, door to door. What's not to like? Regis in 2020!

R **is for Reince Priebus.** The first time I heard the words *Reince Priebus*, I thought it was a skin condition, like shingles or eczema. Turns out, I was right. Every time I see him I start to itch.

"Reince" is an unusual name. According to his family members, their heritage is German and—shockingly!—Russian. Not only is "Reince" an unusual name, but it's hard to pronounce. "Reince" rhymes with "Heinz" (and "Priebus" rhymes with "Ass-Kissing Sycophantic Party Hack"). If my family name were "Priebus" and I had a child, "Reince" wouldn't be on the short list of baby names. It wouldn't be on the long list, either. In fact, it would never cross my mind. I understand and appreciate ethnic pride, but you know what I appreciate more? Common sense. You know full well that every single day of Reince Priebus's life, when he's been introduced to someone, he has had to spend five minutes saying, "No, it's pronounced

Reinz," or, "No, my parents didn't drink," or, "No, I'm not joking," or, "Yes, fine, whatever. It's okay to call me Bob. A lot of people do." Takes the starch right out of that opening conversation, doesn't it?

When Reince was in middle school, he probably had his lunch money stolen at least three times a week. When he was born, his parents should have thought ahead and named him Joey or Steve or Peter. "Peter Priebus" would have made him popular; it sounds vaguely Spiderman-ish.

My parents were Italian—my father was actually born in Italy, but at no point did he and my mother consider naming me "Pinocchio" or "Ismerelda" And they definitely wouldn't have named me "Reince."

I have to take a break now and get some Benadryl. My Reince Priebus is starting to itch and I want to stop it before it spreads to my Orrin Hatch.

R is for Repeat. During the 2008 campaign, Katie Couric famously asked Sarah Palin what newspapers she read, and the Wit from Wasilla was left speechless. I'm not sure if Sarah was stunned because she didn't read newspapers or because she didn't even know what newspapers were. Either way, she was baffled, and referred to it as a "gotcha question." (To me, a gotcha question is "What was the mathematical formula Robert Oppenheimer used to invent the atomic bomb?" or, "If there were sales at both Chico's and Talbots, which store would you go to first?") During the debates, when Trump was asked a gotcha question (which is any question that requires actual knowledge of anything), he either ignored the question or gave a response that had nothing to do with the question asked. And the moderators let him get away with it.

"Mr. Trump, do you have any plans on how to resolve the conflict in Syria?"

"I like soup."

"Thank you, Mr. Trump. Next question . . ."

What they should have done is ask the same question over and over and over again until he answered it, and not ask a different question until he did. Just keep repeating the question. For example, "Mr. Trump, would you or any of the voices in your head be willing to undergo a mental health test to see if you're fit to hold office?"

R is for Reporters. Contrary to what Reichsmarschall Bannon and his boss say, the press is not the "enemy of the people." It's the *voice* of the people. Reporters are *supposed to* ask questions of the government on our behalf, and to hold truth to power. (FYI: I hate the expression "truth to power"; it's so annoying. It's like TV commercials that use the expressions "tasty nougats," "new and improved," or "that not-so-fresh-feeling.")

I put "supposed to" in italics for a reason: it's because during the 2016 presidential campaign, some of the reporters didn't ask the questions they should have or do their jobs as well as they could have. Had they done so, maybe Donald Trump would still be living in New York, shopping for wife number four, and bilking students, vendors, and contractors out of their hard-earned money instead of living in Washington setting our precarious democracy on fire.

For all Trump's bluster about how much he hates the media—he *doesn't*. He needs press coverage the way Dracula needs blood. Maybe if we make him look in a mirror, or go outside on a really, really, really sunny day . . .

I remember one of the first press conferences Trump held early on in the campaign. It was shortly after he started calling Mexicans thugs and rapists. Univision reporter Jorge Ramos stood up to ask him a question about those remarks, and rather than answer the question, Trump had Ramos thrown out of the press conference—he literally had security pull him out of the room. (Afterward, Trump said he had no idea who the security guard was who grabbed Ramos. That, of course, was a lie; the security guard was part of Trump's team.) What happened next was even more appalling: nothing. The press conference went on as though nothing had happened; as though Ramos hadn't been accosted and free speech quashed. In my not-so-humble opinion, every reporter in that room should have gotten up, walked out, and left Trump standing there by himself talking to folding chairs. I'm a comedian, not a journalist, but if I can walk out on Bill O'Reilly—okay, maybe I needed the exercise—certainly they could've mustered the backbone to walk out on Trump when he had their colleague accosted. And they should have walked out of every other subsequent event, rally, and speech when Trump started insulting them, disparaging them, and implying that violence against them was acceptable. Not out of spite, but out of self-preservation. The only thing a narcissist craves is attention. Take attention away from the narcissistic bully, and watch him come crawling back. (I would've liked to see him try to throw Oprah out of a room. Gayle would have kicked his ass from here to Mar-a-Lago.)

R is for Restiva. The drug Restiva apparently cures "dry eye." This must be for those times when Visine, onions, horseradish, and a knee in the nuts for men just won't do the trick. The only person I ever met who had chronically dry eyes was the lady down the hall from me in apartment 7F. She'd had so much plastic surgery she couldn't blink anymore. (She also couldn't smile, frown, sneeze, or cough.) That woman was practically mummified.

The thing that bothers me about Restiva is that the actresses who play the eye doctors in the commercials are all supermodel gorgeous. I'm not saying this doesn't happen in real life, but my ophthalmologist, Dr. Bernstein, is bald except for the hair in his ears and the hump on his back. In all the years I've been going to him, not once have I ever thought, *Thank God I don't have dry eyes. Otherwise, I wouldn't be able to fixate on Dr. B's tight abs and ample package.*

But the most upsetting thing about the Restiva situation (as well as the restless leg meds) is that if the Republicans get their new health care plan in place, probably none of those drugs or doctor's visits will be covered. Which means I'll be sitting in a restaurant surrounded by people shaking their legs and rubbing horseradish in their eyes. Very hard to enjoy chicken marsala with Blinky and Shaky crying and rattling all the other tables.

R is for Restless Leg Syndrome. Restless leg syndrome is a disorder that creates an urge to move one's legs. That's not a disorder, that's walking. Complications are daytime sleepiness, irritability, and depression. I thought that was menopause.

How is this a syndrome? Maybe some people are just fidgety. When I was teaching, half the children in the class shook their legs and squirmed around. Usually they had to go to the bathroom, or they'd forgotten their homework, or they were appalled that I'd given them *Portnoy's Complaint* as a reading assignment. Whatever. They didn't have a syndrome; they were just being children.

Now, in 2017, I find myself squirming around and shaking my legs every time Donald Trump appears on TV or opens his mouth. I don't have a syndrome; I have Trumpophobia, a fear that the president might pick up the wrong device and, instead of tweeting, press the nuclear button. I'm pretty sure there's no medication for that.

R is for Revenge Porn. Over the past few years, a new phenomenon called "revenge porn" has, pardon the double entendre, popped up. This is when a couple breaks up and one of the exes gets so mad he posts nude pics or sex tapes of the other one online.

I find this quite shocking. First of all, unless you're a Kardashian or a model with a rare skin rash posing for a medical journal, what kind of person would let someone take nude pictures of her, let alone videos? In order for a man to see me naked, I have to be in his will. And what kind of a spiteful jerk would get so upset over being dumped that he'd post those pictures and videos online?

Donald Trump would, that's who. He engages in revenge porn without the porn. (I pray that's actually true—the sight of Donald Trump naked is one of those things you can't unsee, like an autopsy photo or Mitch McConnell naked.) Trump is the most spiteful person I've ever seen, and I've seen *a lot* of spiteful people. I've been on *The View* for twenty years, don't forget. I think one of the real reasons Trump fired James Comey is because Comey wouldn't file criminal charges against Hillary Clinton and "lock 'er up!" Trump hates Hillary because she beat him in the popular vote, so he wants whatever revenge he can exact. Yes, Trump has the job, and yes, Republican gerrymandering gave him the Electoral College vote, but he knows full well that she beat him. And he can't let go of it. I just pray that none of his wives ever lets him walk into the bedroom wearing nothing but a camera around his neck.

R **is for Right to Life.** Republicans say they believe in the right to life, but that's not true. They believe in the right to life only for the *un*born (might-possibly-grow-up-to-be-a-Republican-voter-someday), not for the *already* born. They can't cut funding fast enough for prenatal care, postnatal care, maternity leave, health insurance, after-school programs, Head Start, and on and on and on. They're not that keen on living *adults*, either. They oppose the American Jobs Act and want to get rid of labor unions; they oppose most veterans' benefits; they oppose LGBTQ hate crimes and worker protection legislation; they oppose universal health care . . . and on and on and on. The minute you come out of the womb, they drop you like a hot rock.

It also drives me crazy when the Republicans refer to liberals as being "pro-abortion." Nobody I know is "pro-abortion." We're prochoice, and it's not the same thing. I have yet to meet the woman who wakes up in the morning and can't decide whether to go to Costco, take a Pilates class, or have an abortion. I am prochoice, and I choose to have Republicans stay away from my uterus. (Yes, I'm past my childbearing years, but that's not the point. Whether I use that space to house a fetus or store a winter coat, it's none of Newt Gingrich's business.)

R is for **Right-Wing Radio.** In the 1980s, I had my own talk show on WABC Radio in New York. WABC was a right-wing talk station then—believe it or not, my show was on the air every day right before Rush Limbaugh's show. My office was to the left of his—or should I say "far left"? Anyway, Monday through Friday, I'd go on the air and drive WABC's right-wing listeners nuts. I'd do crazy things, like cite facts to support my opinions. This made them furious. Then Rush would come on with his propaganda and soothe the savage beasts. In hindsight, I think Rush owes me a big thank-you for his ratings, because I got the WABC base so angry that when he came on, it was like make-up sex. And everyone likes make-up sex.

Okay, maybe not with Rush Limbaugh, but you get my point. So, Rush, you're welcome.

There is no real left-wing counterbalance to right-wing radio. It's been tried. For a few years, Air America attempted to fill the void on the left, but it never gained support. I think I've finally figured out why. According to *Forbes* magazine, it's all to do with demographics. Most right-wing radio listeners are old white guys with nothing to do but complain. The liberal base is not only much more diverse (with a choice of diverse radio stations to listen to), but most of *our* old, white guys are doing things—volunteering, engaging in social activism, holding their wives' pocketbooks in front of shoe stores in the mall. Whatever pursuit they choose, or have chosen for them, the result is that they're too busy to sit around listening to crabby loudmouths on the radio.

R **is for Eleanor Roosevelt.** Eleanor Roosevelt was our country's longest-serving and most influential First Lady. (And I say that with all due respect to Jackie Kennedy, Betty Ford, Michelle Obama, and Martha Washington, who not only was our *first* First Lady, but spent almost every night for four years picking splinters out of her thighs.) Eleanor Roosevelt became a spokesperson for human rights and women's rights, championed the plight of the poor, and was a beacon of strength during World War II and the Great Depression. (I hate calling that period of American history the "Great Depression." To me, it's an oxymoron. It's like saying, "excellent emphysema" or "pretty polyps.")

Eleanor wrote daily news columns and hosted radio shows; she was ahead of her time. In fact, if Eleanor were alive today, she'd be all over Instagram and Snapchat, and she'd be tweeting Trump right off Twitter. I think Eleanor would have been horrified by Trump. Trump makes fun of the disabled; FDR was disabled. Also, when Trump cheated on his wives with a new girlfriend, an ugly divorce ensued. When Franklin cheated on Eleanor with a new girlfriend, she didn't divorce him; she just got a new girlfriend, too. (Allegedly.)

R is for Rose Garden. The White House Rose Garden, which borders the Oval Office, is one of the most iconic places in the country. It has been the site of so many important events— JFK welcoming home the Mercury astronauts, Tricia Nixon's wedding, the 1994 Israel-Jordan Peace Treaty signing, and, most recently, the installation of a secret trap door that leads to the tunnel to get to the Kremlin.

R is for Rosie O'Donnell. You'd think Donald Trump and Rosie O'Donnell would get along. They're both New Yorkers, they're both TV stars, and they both have five children with three different women. But no, Trump hates her.

You may recall that, back in the day, and on *The View*, Rosie made fun of Trump's hair, his finances (or lack thereof), and his adulterous behavior. This sent The Donald into paroxysms of vituperative insults. He called Rosie every name in the book—a "slob," "disgusting" with a "fat, ugly face."

This is known as an ad hominem attack, meaning it's personal, not political, and looked upon as a low blow and not becoming of a mature person. Let's remember that Trump is the king of ad hominem. Trump called Marco Rubio "dumb," Ted Cruz was "lyin' Ted," Bernie Sanders was "crazy," and Elizabeth Warren, "goofy." But it seems that The Donald has a special hatred in his heart for Rosie.

Why? My opinion is that she is a *woman* who spoke the truth and mocked him in front of millions of people—yes, *The View* has millions of viewers, and good ratings—and Tiny Hands's fragile ego could not deal with that. I've noticed that he becomes particularly unhinged when women go after him (Megyn Kelly, Carly Fiorina, and of course that "nasty woman" Hillary Rodham Clinton). It's been ten years since that infamous exchange between him and O'Donnell, but in May 2017, after he fired FBI director James Comey, he tweeted, "We finally agree on something, Rosie." (Apparently, Rosie had been in favor of firing Comey because of the way he'd handled the Clinton email debacle.)

Let's pause here to absorb the fact that the leader of the free world, the man who complains that he cannot get his agenda going because of ongoing investigations, is obsessing over Rosie O'Donnell. He's too "busy" to go to briefings or read up on history, yet he apparently took the time out of his sleepless nights to wander around the West Wing in his bathrobe, searching for Rosie's tweet about Comey, and then post it, as if this validated his decision to fire the FBI director.

Now I'm waiting for Trump to locate something that *I've* tweeted to validate a decision he's made. I could be responsible indirectly for World War III. His tweet will say, "Joy Behar finally agrees with me on something, so let's just take out North Korea."

R is for Russian Hacking. The first time I heard "Russian hack" on TV, I thought, *Is Yakov Smirnoff still working?* But then I realized they were talking about a foreign power breaking into our secure computer networks, and I felt so much better.

The issue of Russia hacking into our computers became a huge talking point during the debates between Secretary of State Clinton and game show host Donald Trump. Clinton pointed out that the Russians hacked our computers to help the Trump campaign because Putin wanted a puppet in the White House. In response, Trump started whining, "I'm no puppet, you're the puppet. You're the puppet!" I'm betting that Trump *is* Putin's puppet—it would certainly explain why he has Putin's hand up his ass. If I'm wrong, however, then Trump's not Putin's puppet; he's Putin's bitch. Either way, at least now he's prepped for a colonoscopy.

R is for *To Россия with Love*. I don't understand Trump's obsession with Russia. I find it more confusing than Sudoku. I don't know much about Russia (which, of course, would qualify me to be Trump's ambassador to Russia), other than that they make good vodka, fur hats, and great pairs figure skating teams. I *do* know, however, that Russia and the United States have not been allies since the end of World War

II. Tensions ramped up during the Cold War, and we've been monitoring their nuclear capabilities for decades. Oh, I also know that Vladimir Putin is an authoritarian, and that a lot of his political enemies (real or perceived), including the press, tend to wind up missing or dead. Not exactly a Tinder profile I'd swipe right on.

Yet, Trump seems to love both Russia and Putin. He says Putin was a better leader than Obama. He says Putin is strong and tough. Trump has said Putin is a "tough guy," "he's 'brilliant.'" He even claimed that Putin had complimented him and called him "a genius." Who could resist that? Trump told right-wing radio mouthpiece Michael Savage that he met Putin "a long time ago . . . and we got along great, by the way." Sounds like quite a first date.

So, Donnie, why all the props for Putin? Do you and he share a love that dare not speak its name? Is he really Vlad the Impaler? And more important, does Mike Pence know?

I'm kidding of course. I don't think Trump and Putin are lovers. (I've seen Vlad half-naked on a horse, and I doubt he'd be into the Pillsbury Doughboy.) I think Trump is just impressed with unquestioned, unbridled dictatorial power, which would also explain his bizarre man-crushes on the strongmen leaders Recep Tayyip Erdogan of Turkey, Xi Jinping of China, Rodrigo Duterte of the Philippines, and Abdel Fattah el-Sisi of Egypt. I don't think he's having affairs with any of them, either. (Although, if they compliment him enough, who knows?) I just think he has lust in his heart (with sincere apologies to Jimmy Carter). He's attracted to the idea of total, uncontested power with no obstacles or pesky Constitutions annoying him. He had all that on his reality show, and he now thinks the Oval Office is the "boardroom" on *The Apprentice*.

The other reason for Trump's obsession with the Head of Red is green. I was watching CNN today, and it seems that when it comes to money, The Donald and the Kremlin are closer than cousins in West Virginia. Trump acolytes Carter Page, Paul Manafort, and Michael Flynn—or, as I think of them, the Nuclear Triad—are all very closely connected to Russia in that they seem to have had shady relationships with shady people who are all shadily connected to Putin.

This does not seem to bother Trump's diehard supporters in the least. But it should. Let's get something straight here: Russia is not a friend of the United States. We're not even frenemies. You know that type of rich woman with the stretched skin, who gives air kisses when she runs into an "old friend" at a restaurant and says, "OMG, Marion, you look great. We'll have to get together soon," when in fact she's been schtupping Marion's husband in the pool house for six months?

What upsets me even more than Trump's dry-humping our enemies is his antagonistic treatment of our allies, including England, Germany, Australia, and even Canada, for God's sake. How do you pick a fight with Justin Trudeau? He's the kind of man you hope your daughter will marry. He's the kind of man you hope your *son* will marry. God forbid anything ever happened to my husband. Once I got over my grief, I'm pretty sure I'd be heading up to Ottawa for a little *voulez-vous* with Monsieur Trudeau.

S is for Sad! When The Donald is in his tweeting mode (usually in the middle of the night), his favorite word seems to be *sad*. Here are just a *few* tweets, sent during the first two months of the 2016 campaign:

Mar. 3

@realDonaldTrump

Because of me, the Republican Party has taken in millions of new voters, a record. If they are not careful, they will all leave. Sad!

Feb. 28

@realDonaldTrump

@fairess369: It is a sad commentary little boy Marco Rubio can't win in his home state. Floridians despise him as a opportunist phony.

Feb. 24

@realDonaldTrump

The polls show that I picked up many Jeb Bush supporters. That is how I got to 46%. When others drop out, I will pick up more. Sad but true

Feb. 22

@realDonaldTrump

Ted Cruz should be disqualified from his fraudulent win in Iowa. Weak RNC and Republican leadership probably won't let this happen! Sad.

The Great Gasbag

Feb. 20
@realDonaldTrump

I wonder if President Obama would have attended the funeral of Justice Scalia if it were held in a Mosque? Very sad that he did not go!

Feb. 13
@realDonaldTrump

I am the only one who can fix this. Very sad. Will not happen under my watch! #MakeAmericaGreatAgain

Feb. 12
@realDonaldTrump

Lightweight @JebBush is spending a fortune of special interest against me in SC. False advertising-desperate and sad!

Feb. 8
@realDonaldTrump

Now that Bush has wasted $120 million of special interest money on his failed campaign, he says he would end super PACs. Sad!

Jan. 23
@realDonaldTrump

The only reason irrelevant @GlennBeck doesn't like me is I refused to do his failing show—asked many times. Very few listeners—sad!

Jan. 22

@realDonaldTrump

> National Review is a failing publication that has lost it's
> way. It's circulation is way down w its influence being at
> an all time low. Sad!

Jan. 21

@realDonaldTrump

> So sad that @CNN and many others refused to show
> the massive crowd at the arena yesterday in Oklahoma.
> Dishonest reporting!

Jan. 21

@realDonaldTrump

> Wacko @glennbeck is a sad answer to the
> @SarahPalinUSA endorsement that Cruz so desperately
> wanted. Glenn is a failing, crying, lost soul!

Jan. 13

@realDonaldTrump

> Sadly, there is no way that Ted Cruz can continue
> running in the Republican Primary unless he can erase
> doubt on eligibility. Dems will sue!

Jan. 7

@realDonaldTrump

> The @TheView @ABC, once great when headed by
> @BarbaraJWalters, is now in total freefall. Whoopi
> Goldberg is terrible. Very sad!

Jan. 2

@realDonaldTrump. @JebBush is a sad case. A total embarrassment to both himself and his family, he just announced he will continue to spend on Trump hit ads!

You know what's really sad? That a seventy-year-old man is awake at all hours of the night, tweeting mean things about more well-adjusted people who are probably sleeping. You know what's even sadder? The fact that a seventy-year-old man doesn't own a thesaurus. Here are some synonyms for *sad*:

Unhappy (your wife Melania)

Miserable (your disposition)

Dismal (your legislative record, so far)

Despicable (your sons' hunting trips)

Tragic (your administration)

Unfortunate (your election)

Cheerless (your personality)

Morose (your PR staff)

Sorrowful (your voters)

Bitter (you)

Deplorable (ask Hillary)

S is for Santorum. Aside from Mike Let's-Do-Conversion-Therapy-Even-If-They're-Not-Gay Pence, Rick Santorum is possibly the most homophobic politico in the country. My favorite Santorum statement is "I have no problem with homosexuality. I have a problem with homosexual acts."

Okay, here's the deal, Ricky. Liza Minnelli is a gay act. A blow job is just a blow job. Are we clear?

S is for Science. Republicans in Congress hate science. They much prefer to use God, Jesus, miracles, or magic to explain things—or not to pay for things. For example, anytime a piece of environmental legislation comes up that might cost their corporate donors a dollar, Republicans in Congress like to say, "Well, I'm not a scientist, so I don't know that that's true." Climate change? "Well, I'm not a scientist . . ." News flash: I'm not a scientist, either, but I go outside sometimes. And when it's six hundred degrees in March, there are so many tornadoes that Kansas is now in Virginia, hurricane season is twelve months long, and it hasn't rained in California since the gold rush, I don't need a degree in physics or meteorology to know there's a problem—all I need is a window.

Marco Rubio and Rick Scott love to point out that they're not scientists. They're not Olympic swimmers, either, which might be problematic when Florida's underwater in a few years. Vice Homophobe Mike Pence is another big science denier (shocking!). He's not sure about evolution, he doesn't believe in climate change, and in 1998 he wrote an op-ed piece in which he said, "Despite the hysteria from the political class and the media, smoking doesn't kill." Yo, Mikey, the hysteria didn't come from the middle class and the media. It came from the surgeon general of the United States, fifty years ago. (FYI: Pence has received more than one hundred thousand dollars from the tobacco industry in his political career, and gutted as much antismoking legislation as he could when he was governor of Indiana. So, he may not be a doctor or a scientist, but that doesn't stop him from standing by his "alternative facts." Question: is he investing in inhalers and respirators? Just askin'.)

S is for Scott Baio. Thank God for Donald Trump. There, I've said it. As a result, my tongue is swelling and my throat's closing, so I'd better explain before I get cast as a corpse on *Criminal Minds*. For years, I've been beside myself worrying about what happened to Chachi. I can't tell you how many mornings I'd wake up with this dark cloud hanging over me. My husband would say, "Joy, are you okay?" I'd say nothing, and he'd look at me knowingly and say, "Chachi, again?" And I'd just nod and start weeping gently, wiping my tears on the Slanket I bought on QVC for $29.95.

is for **Secrets**. This White House keeps more secrets than a Scientologist returning to the mothership after a weekend on Fire Island.

The last big thing Scott Baio did was *Charles in Charge*, which went off the air in 1990. I know, I know, he's done a bunch of guest roles on TV and had a series on Nickelodeon, but it's not the same. I realize that following a seminal piece of theatrical work like *Charles in Charge* isn't easy, and Nickelodeon is better than playing Biff in a dinner theater production of *Death of a Salesman* in Sheboygan, but still, we're talking about Scott Fucking Baio here.

Then, along comes Donald Trump, and out of oblivion comes Scott Baio. I don't know if Trump had any idea who Scott Baio was, but since he was having trouble getting celebrities to endorse him, suddenly Donnie Loves Chachi. (Trump couldn't even get an endorsement from the chair that Clint Eastwood spoke to.)

Lo and behold, Scott Baio gets a speaking role at the 2016 Republican National Convention. When he walked onstage, the crowd went wild—apparently, just like me, they, too, had been worried about him, not having seen him in years. (There was even a rumor that he had fallen down a well like Baby Jessica, but that nobody in Hollywood wanted to look for him.) I was thrilled to see my Scottie, but then . . . he began to speak. And it turns out, just like his Trump, he doesn't know anything. He thinks "Make America Great Again" is a policy plan, not a slogan on a hat. He said he thought President Obama was either dumb or a Muslim. He said Donald Trump made him proud to be an American again.

I turned off the TV and went back to bed, gently weeping.

And when my husband said, "Chachi, again?" I said, "Yes." But this time, not because I didn't know what had happened to him, but because I did.

S is for Secrets. This White House keeps more secrets than a Scientologist returning to the mothership after a weekend on Fire Island. There are only three real reasons for secrecy: (a) you're doing something wrong; (b) you're throwing a surprise party, or (c) you don't want to hurt someone's feelings. We know it's not *c*. I can't imagine it's *b*, because what are the odds Trump would throw a party for anyone but himself? Which leaves us with *a*, "you're doing something wrong," or, in Trump's case, *everything* wrong. He won't release his taxes, he won't tell us his plans for combatting terrorism, he launches strikes and drops bombs without consulting Congress, he issues mini-nonstatements about meetings with world leaders, he releases a vague tax "plan" that's shorter than my grocery list, and on and on and on. All presidents keep some things secret—President Obama closed the drapes when he was smoking cigarettes; President Clinton closed the drapes when Monica was smoking him; President Reagan shut the door when he was trading arms for hostages; President Cheney sealed the windows when he was ginning up the war in Iraq. But given Trump's history of deceit—Trump U, anyone?—his level of secrecy is both expected and appalling at the same time. As an American citizen, I'd like some explanations for what he's doing—or at least some alternative explanations.

S is for Seriously versus Literally. Trump supporters say he should be taken seriously but not literally. So, if, for example, Trump casually says, "I'm going to drop a nuclear bomb on One Hundred Thirty-Sixth Street and Amsterdam Avenue, right by City College in Upper Manhattan," are we not supposed to take that literally? Should the students just shrug it off with a wry smile and an "Oh, that Donald, what a kidder"? If we don't take him literally, does that mean it might not be a nuclear bomb, but just a garden-variety napalm bomb? Or does it mean he's not going bomb 136th Street, but might bomb 134th Street, or maybe just some other block in the neighborhood? I take Trump both literally *and* seriously. But what I'd like to do is take him to Russia . . . and leave him there.

S is for Shame. Last week, my husband and I had some friends over to our house for dinner, and eventually the conversation turned to Trump. And by "eventually," I mean, during the appetizers. My friend Susie couldn't even wait until the chicken cutlets were served to start in. That day, like nearly every other day, Trump had said something crude, vulgar, mean-spirited, and patently false. Susie was upset by it, and after two cocktails and a crab cake—she's gluten-free, of course—she was outraged. "The man ought to be ashamed of himself," she yelled. My friend Larry replied, "That would imply he has a sense of shame, but apparently Trump was born without that gene."

An example of something that causes shame: Your doctor

tells you to lose fifty pounds, and at your next checkup, he notices you've gained eight pounds and you have an entire brisket stuck between your teeth.

What has Donald Trump done that should have caused him to feel shame? Let me count the ways:

- Publicly cheated on his wives
- Defrauded people out of money
- Bankrupted business associates
- Bragged about sexually assaulting women
- Defamed his opponents
- Made false claims about his predecessor
- Denigrated a war hero
- Insulted the Pope
- Mocked the disabled
- Lied about mocking the disabled

. . . and yet, he's not ashamed of any of it. So, he either doesn't know those things are wrong, or he doesn't think he did them. Either way, does this sound like someone who should be in the White House? This isn't someone I'd let in my house—although, if I did, I'd make sure Susie was there, too, just to watch the fireworks over dessert (which would contain no carbs and would be gluten-free, of course).

S is for Social Conservatives. I refuse to refer to the self-righteous, ultra-tight-ass wing of the Republican Party as "social conservatives." People who don't like the way other people live their lives and try to deny them the same rights that they freely enjoy aren't social conservatives; they're intolerant. You want to talk social conservative? My aunt Viola, now *she* was a social conservative. She wore a bra and panties under her bathing suit when she went to the beach, so "men wouldn't look." (Not for nothing, but my aunt Viola weighed four hundred pounds—the only man looking at her longingly was the ice-cream vendor.) A social conservative is a guy who stubs his toe and says, "Oh, fudge," instead of "Fuck me. How did I not see that chair?" A person who says, "I don't want to bake cakes for gay people," isn't a social conservative; he's a lousy businessman.

S is for Sociopath. My friend Terry is a practicing clinical psychologist. She's listened to more people complain than a customer service rep at the DMV. She's convinced that Donald Trump displays classic signs of sociopathy. Some of the characteristics of being a sociopath are: a disregard for the feelings of others, a lack of shame or remorse, a huge ego, compulsive lying to achieve one's goals, manipulative behavior, and making statements that may incite violence. Now, I'm no psychiatrist, so I'm going to make like Fox News: I present the facts; you decide. And if your conclusion scares you, I'll give you Terry's number.

S is for Son of Sam. In 1976 to '77, New York City was paralyzed with fear by a maniac known as the Son of Sam, a serial killer who was traveling around the five boroughs randomly shooting young couples. Berkowitz became known as the Son of Sam when, after his arrest, he told the police that he was killing people under orders from his neighbor Sam's dog. I don't know if the dog actually spoke to him; I don't even know if the dog even spoke, but if it did, I hope that dog is still alive, because I'll call Simon Cowell and put him on *America's Got Talent* and collect me a nice little finder's fee. (On a side note, why is that when people hear voices, those voices always tell them to kill? How come those voices never say things like "Mow the lawn" or "Take out the garbage" or "Buy Joy a lovely bracelet at Neiman Marcus"?)

Berkowitz killed six people and wounded seven others because he took advice from "someone" ill-equipped to give advice: Sam's dog. Donald Trump has put someone equally ill-equipped to give advice to run the Department of Energy: Rick Perry. The Department of Energy is responsible for our nuclear arsenal. Prior to being named secretary of energy, Rick Perry (a) had no idea what the department actually did; (b) said he wanted to dismantle it when he was running for president himself in 2012; and (c) appeared on *Dancing with the Stars*. The only differences between Rick Perry and that pooch who spoke to David Berkowitz is that Rick Perry is housebroken *and* he's in a position to end a lot more than six lives.

S is for Spine. Years ago, a very funny comedian named Marvin Braverman was sitting in a crowded cinema watching the premiere of the movie *The Elephant Man*. In a pivotal scene, the Elephant Man, John Merrick, twisted and disfigured, finds himself at a tailor's, trying on a suit. As he stands in front of the three-sided mirror, he says to the tailor, "How do I look?"

With the theater audience totally silent, Marvin yelled out from his seat, "The truth?"

I know. Inappropriate, but funny and honest.

Which brings me to Mitch McConnell and Paul Ryan, who know full well that Donald Trump is a train wreck driving our democracy off the rails. Yet, they do nothing but acquiesce and capitulate to President Crazypants's whims. They need to take a page from Marvin Braverman, who had the cojones to yell out the truth.

S is for Stock Market. One of the things Donald Trump likes to take credit for is the rising stock market. What he doesn't mention is that he inherited a booming stock market from President Obama, a market that kept reaching record highs. He keeps telling his base that the market numbers show how great he's doing. They, of course, believe him. The irony is that the majority of his hard-core base probably doesn't own stocks. They don't play the stock market; they go to the supermarket. Their daily lives are more affected by the numbers at Piggly Wiggly than the numbers at NASDAQ. I hope they figure that out. So, to you Trump diehards out there (all two of you who bought this book), remember that the price of Apple is not going to help you with the price of apples.

S is for Style. Why do all tyrants have bad hair and terrible fashion sense? I don't get it. They're the most powerful people in their countries, yet they can't find one person who knows how to cut hair or put together an outfit?

Hitler was usually to be found wearing a brown Nazi uniform. Admittedly, the red armband added a pop of color, but brown was *soooo* 1922. The Führer's hair and mustache were flat-out awful, too. First of all, it was a bad cut, cropped short near the ears with one long bang hanging down the side. Even worse, it was greasy. On a hot day, you could cook a schnitzel on his head. And the mustache? How did that even start? Was he grooming one morning and suddenly had to stop mid-shave when Eva Braun marched in dangling a whip and some handcuffs? It was such a bad mustache. I've never, ever seen any other human being wearing it, and that includes my aunt Annunziata.

Good thing they don't have much electricity in North Korea. Kim Jong-un looks best in bad light. As a chubbette, he faces certain challenges, but that hairdo is not going to make his face look any less round. The only thing that would elongate Kim's face is a feedbag. His outside is as bad as his inside. As they say in Sicily, *faccia brutta*.

Even Ghaddafi tried to enhance his façade by wrapping what he considered a stunning schmata on his head. And Mussolini, to his credit, knew enough to shave his pate so as to avoid the dreaded male-pattern baldness fringe.

I have no idea if Hitler thought he looked nice, or if Kim Jong-un thinks he is the Fabio of Pyongyang, but Donald Trump clearly thinks of himself as a hottie. Donald must spend copious amounts of time fixing the 'do, spraying on the orange tan, Turtle Waxing the teeth, and making sure his tie is long enough to cover his gut. Maybe that's why he's up at 3:00 in the morning, tweeting: he's under the dryer starting his daily beauty regimen.

If I were The Donald, I'd either (a) start earlier, or (b) start over. If Trump spent less time brushing his hair and more time brushing up on facts, the country might start looking better.

S is for Superlatives. As I've already mentioned, Donald Trump loves hyperbole. But not just any old hyperbole—the greatest, the finest, the best hyperbole. And that's no exaggeration.

S is for Supreme Court. I never thought my civil rights, my daughter's civil rights, and my grandson's civil rights would hinge on the continuing good health of an eighty-four-year-old Jewish woman from Brooklyn, Ruth Bader Ginsburg. (If I had known that old age was the criterion, I'd have asked Bill Clinton to nominate my mother's friend Estelle Weinstein to the Court. Estelle is indefatigable. The woman never sleeps; she plays mah-jongg 24 hours a day, 365 days a year, even on Rosh Hashanah and Yom Kippur, and almost always wins.)

During the campaign, some of my friends said they were

going to sit out the election because they hated Trump and didn't like Hillary. I told them that their vote was important, if for no other reason than that a seat on the Supreme Court was open (and had been kept open by that great constitutionalist Mitch McConnell, who had changed the very document he "so reveres" to suit his agenda). Hillary would have nominated a better candidate than Trump. And now that Trump is in the White House, and Neil Gorsuch is on the Supreme Court, I say to my friends who sat out the election, "Happy now? When Gorsuch overturns *Roe v. Wade* and you get pregnant, don't come crying to me." Of course, most of these women are in their sixties, so if they get pregnant, they shouldn't call me. They should call Ripley's.

Neil Gorsuch believes corporations are people, and he overwhelmingly rules in their favor in his decisions and opinions. If Joseph and Mary had been busted for squatting in the manger, Gorsuch would have ruled in favor of the slumlord who ran that condemned barn, thrown the Three Wise Men in jail for trespassing, and sent Jesus to foster care.

S is for Surrogate. These days, when people hear the word *surrogate*, they probably think of a pretty but strapped-for-cash girl from Oklahoma carrying a baby for some good-looking couple from San Francisco. But when I hear the word *surrogate*, I think of the cadre of Kool-Aid-drinking sycophants who speak on Donald Trump's behalf, primarily his rotating corps of spokespeople. The original mouthpiece who made a deal with the devil was Kellyanne Conway, whom I've already discussed ad nauseam, with an emphasis on the "nauseam." Then there was Stephen Miller, one of Trump's right-wing policy wonks, who was so hateful and offensive he was dragged off the national stage faster than passengers get dragged off United Airlines flights. Then came my favorite explainer-du-jour, Sean Spicer. I was going to say "apologist-du-jour," but as previously noted, Trump never apologizes for anything, so "explainer" will have to do.

I've got to be honest: I got a certain pleasure out of watching Sean Spicer try to stammer his way through a press conference. Every time he was asked to explain one of Trump's lies, he stammered and cajoled and deflected. It reminded me of when I begged my calculus teacher for a D so I could graduate. But as much as I enjoyed the schadenfreude I experienced when Sean got caught in a lie, I also felt sorry for him. Unlike Stephen Miller, who is a true believer, and Kellyanne, who is a paid believer, I get the impression Sean Spicer knew that what he was saying was complete bullshit but that he had to say it anyway. Plus, we all know that Spicer was speaking to an audience of one, and if he didn't answer correctly, he might have ended up in Guantánamo. Couple that with the fact that Spicer, not unlike his boss, is factually challenged, and every press conference turned into Must See TV. And that's what Trump wants in a press secretary: high ratings!

Here are some of the actual things Sean Spicer said in public (or, as I like to call them, "Spicerisms"):

- Magnetometers kept crowds off the Mall at the inauguration (not true).

- A new style of ground covering made it appear as though the crowd was sparse (not true).

- The DC subway rider usage numbers proved that Trump's was the largest inauguration crowd ever (not true).

- Paul Manafort played a very limited role (in the campaign) for a very limited time (not true).

- Even Hitler didn't sink to using chemical weapons (not true).

From what I hear, Sean Spicer was even more of a hot mess offstage. Here are some of the Spicerisms uttered in private:

- Sean Hannity's IQ is higher than Stephen Hawking's.

- Andrea Mitchell's feet are made out of liverwurst.

- There are Islamic terrorists hiding in Abe Lincoln's nose on Mount Rushmore.

- Susan Sarandon is a Cuban spy named Raúl.

- President Duterte of the Philippines is on the short list for canonization.

T is for Tammy Wynette. Country star Tammy Wynette's biggest hit song was "Stand by Your Man," which became an anthem for subservient women stoically staying in bad, sexless marriages. Think of poor Pat Nixon in her cloth coat, a flask in her purse, standing beside Tricky Dick while he sweated his way through press conferences telling people he was not a crook. Pat stood by her man (the way Melania is standing by her man), even when Dick had to resign the presidency before being impeached. I can only pray that Melania shows the same courage Pat displayed, when her Donald is forced to resign before *he's* impeached. FYI: Tammy Wynette may have sung that anthem, but she was no dummy. She was married eight times.

T is for Taxes. To Donald Trump, *taxes* is a dirty word, one of the few dirty words he hates to use. Trump's tax returns are harder to find than a period at the end of one of Kellyanne Conway's sentences. During the campaign, Deceptive Donny said he was being audited by the IRS and wasn't allowed to release his taxes until the audit was done. (According to the IRS, not true. FYI: even Nixon, the Sultan of Sneaky, released his taxes while he was under audit *and* under investigation for Watergate.) Then Trump said that the American people "don't care about his taxes." Again, not true. I'm an American people and I care—and according to current polls, so do 72 percent of the rest of the American people. Then his son Benito . . . I mean, Hans, said that his father's tax return was twelve thousand pages and would take too long to go through. Not true.

There are plenty of great accountants with OCD in this country who would be thrilled to read those pages, and who could use the extra work. Even Trump's favorite "intelligence gathering agency," WikiLeaks, thinks something is fishy.

@wikileaks
Trump's breach of promise over the release of his tax returns is even more gratuitous than Clinton concealing her Goldman Sachs transcripts.
9:15 AM—22 Jan 2017

Actually, WikiLeaks is only Donald Trump's fifth-favorite intelligence gathering agency; it comes after Breitbart News, Alex Jones's Infowars, the *National Enquirer*, and the lady he overheard talking to her friend Selma at the airport.

There are a lot of theories as to why Trump won't release his tax returns. I'm going with that he doesn't want us to find out he's claimed Vladimir Putin as a dependent.

T is for Tea Bag. See: "O is for Orange." Though Donald Trump's face is orange, the areas around and under his eyes are pale white. I'm not sure why. I'm guessing he's either part raccoon or he's been tea-bagged by a mime.

T is for Tea Party. The original tea party was a protest where angry citizens dumped tea in Boston Harbor yelling, "No taxation without representation." The Tea Party that emerged in 2009 was composed of angry citizens who stood in parking lots with tea bags on their heads, holding signs saying things against Obama like LIER IN CHEIF and COMMANDER AND THEIF. I don't want to be picky, but it's *i* before *e* except after *c*, or when sounding like *a* as in *neighbor* and *weigh*. So, it's *chief*, not *cheif*, okay? Got that? Next week, we'll go over the use of dangling participles. I promise it won't hurt.

T is for Tea-Bagged. Though Donald Trump's face is orange, the areas around and under his eyes are pale white. I'm not sure why. I'm guessing he's either part raccoon or he's been tea-bagged by a mime.

T is for Teddy Roosevelt. The old Rough Rider was the last Republican president not to have maternal issues. Think about it: Ike had Mamie, Reagan called his wife "Mommy," Bush Sr. married his mommy, W. needed his mommy, and Trump thinks his mother was a 5, maybe a 6.

T is for Ted Nugent. Redneck rocker Ted Nugent was "invited" by the Secret Service for "interviews" at least twice for making threatening and incendiary remarks toward President Obama. After that, any decent, normal elected official would have steered clear of this aging musical misanthrope, if for no other reason than bad optics. But not Donald Trump. He invited Ted to perform at the inauguration. Presumably, that means that Jesse James (Sandra Bullock's ex, who loves Nazi memorabilia) can't hold a tune. (That said, neither can Ted Nougat.)

T is for Temperament. During the 2016 campaign, Hillary and the Democrats kept saying that Trump was "temperamentally unfit for office." In hindsight, they were being way too polite. Hillary should have slipped on her big-boy pantsuit and yelled, "That is one crazy motherfucker!"

T is for Terrible Twos. Toddlers go through a phase at about two years old when they cry, they whine, they break things, they have tantrums, they won't eat, and they throw food. Experts believe the cause of this is that children's brains develop faster than their language skills, and when they can't express what they're thinking, they get frustrated and act out. This phase usually ends at about three years old. Usually. There are exceptions. I know of one world leader who is sixty-eight years late and counting.

T is for Terrorism. During the 2016 election, Candidate Trump told America he was going to get rid of ISIS in his first thirty days in office. Apparently, the calendar app on his iPhone broke. Months later, ISIS is still ticking, and since I have no plans of vacationing in Iran or buying a time share in Syria, I'm more afraid of Trump and Pence than I am of

Sheik Al-Sheik or his kooky nephew Sheik Sheik Sheik Your Booty.

T **is for Tiffany.** Donald named his daughter for his favorite jewelry store, Tiffany. She's lucky he doesn't shop at Hammacher Schlemmer.

T **is for Tiny Hands.** You know what they say about men with tiny hands? Tiny mittens. A lot has been made of the size of Donald Trump's hands and fingers. Critics say they're minute; Trump, of course, says they're *uuuuuge*. My own estimate is that on the size scale, they fall somewhere between stumps and the hands of a small Filipino child. But other than the women whose pussies he plans on grabbing, who cares about the size of his fingers? I don't. I care about the size of his brain, which, sadly, appears to be smaller than his hands.

T **is for Toadies.** Toadies are sycophants who grovel and fawn, give up all sense of pride or self-respect, are humiliated and shit on by the celebrity they're fawning over, get shit on again, and then come back for more. Alternate definition: Chris Christie.

T **is for Toe Fungus.** People keep stopping me on the street and asking me, "Joy, would you rather have Donald Trump as president, or would you rather have toe fungus?" The answer is: Toe fungus. It's curable.

T **is for Trade Agreements.** Donald Trump knows *a lot* about making trades. He traded in Ivana for Marla, and traded in Marla for Melania. (I think Melania's got another twenty thousand miles on her until he trades her in for a newer model.) One of the first things Donald Trump did in office was go after the Trans-Pacific Partnership, or as Bernie Sanders kept yelling, "TPP, TPP!" Let's be honest, Bernie was obsessed. I can't get the image out of my head of him screaming, "TPP, TPP, TPP!" At night, when my husband gets a little too frisky, I yell out, "TPP, TPP!" and we stop and calm down and discuss trade tariffs.

Believe it or not, Bernie and Donald Trump were on the same page when it came to getting out of the TPP. Neither one of them liked it. The only difference is Bernie described it in complex economic terms, while Trump simply called it a "horrible deal." I have no idea what's in the TPP—I haven't read it, and I don't plan to read it. I'm still only halfway through *Fifty Shades of Grey* and I'm not going to put it down to read a government document until the spankings begin.

T **is for Transgender.** Republicans spend more time worrying about other people's junk than Sanford and Son. In April 2016, when Trump was asked about the "transgender bathroom crisis," he said, "People should go to the bathroom where they feel comfortable . . . even in Trump Tower." (Or maybe on a mattress in Moscow?) But in less than a year, in February 2017, he overturned President Obama's law protecting transgender students' right to use the bathroom they feel comfortable in. How is this even an issue? I'd like Trump to name one transgender person who is a national threat.

I only know a few transgender celebrities: Chaz Bono, Caitlyn Jenner, and Laverne Cox. I think Laverne is the only one who has had the full surgery; the others may still be in various stages of transitioning. Chaz (née Chastity) was really brave to be among the first celebrities to publicly come out as gay. Then, a few years later, he came out as transgender. Coming out is a daunting prospect for most young people—I can't imagine how difficult it must be when your mother is Cher. Think about it: Your mother is a big star, an Oscar winner, and a staple in every drag queen's act . . . and you have to come home and tell her you're turning in your ovaries. I was an absolute wreck the day I had to tell my mother I wasn't a virgin. And I was thirty-seven! I give Chaz credit. Good for him.

And I give Caitlyn (née Bruce) Jenner lots of props, too. Again, I'm not sure what stage of the transition Caitlyn is at. She's clearly had hormones and implants. Going from being the best male athlete in the world to being a middle-aged suburban woman takes, pardon the pun, a lot of balls. Caitlyn wasn't just "some guy." When other guys sat down to eat their Wheaties for breakfast, Bruce Jenner was the guy they saw looking out at them from the front of the cereal box. It took a lot of courage for Caitlyn to do what she did. So, my question is: Since the current GOP platform is the most anti-LGBTQ platform *ever*, why is she still a Republican? If Caitlyn had the courage to change genders, I'm sure she has the courage to change parties. Go where you're wanted, Cait! The Democrats would love to have you.

T **is for Trazodone.** My favorite sleeping pill. I'm taking one now. All this Trump talk is giving me agita.

T **is for Tweets and Twits.** Tweeting is a preferred method of communication among middle school and high school students—and between Donald Trump and the American people.

Donald Trump loves tweeting almost as much as he loves himself. Morning, noon, and night, The Donald tweets. The White House is open for tweeting 24/7. It's like a 7-Eleven. Four o'clock in the morning, a time when most seventy-year-old men would be sleeping or counting out Cialis pills, Trump's tiny fingers are flying over those keys like a World War II Luftwaffe pilot. Four in the morning, and Agent Orange is sitting there in his silk pajamas, with the lights on, typing away.

Twitter is perfect for Trump. He can communicate only in 140 characters or less, which breaks down to one character for each of his personalities. Tweeting is also a method of bullying, because you can tweet what you want and have no obligation to read any replies. A nasty tweet is basically a fuck-you, like hanging up on a caller or slamming a door in someone's face. In addition to the sampling of tweets in the *S* section, here are a couple of Trump's especially petty, vindictive, small-minded, childish tweets:

@realDonaldTrump
    . . . John McCain has failed miserably to fix the
    situation and to make it possible for Veterans to
    successfully manage their lives.
11:15 AM—18 Jul 2015

@realDonaldTrump
    I hear that sleepy eyes @chucktodd will be fired like
    a dog from ratings starved Meet The Press? I can't
    imagine what is taking so long!
5:36 PM—12 Jul 2015

@realDonaldTrump
    Meryl Streep, one of the most over-rated actresses in
    Hollywood, doesn't know me but attacked last night at
    the Golden Globes.
3:27 AM—9 Jan 2017

@realDonaldTrump
    @Macys was one of the worst performing stocks on the
    S&P last year, plunging 46%. Very disloyal company.
    Another win for Trump! Boycott.
3:15 AM—7 Jan 2016

@realDonaldTrump
  Did Crooked Hillary help disgusting (check out sex tape
  and past) Alicia M become a U.S. citizen so she could
  use her in the debate?
2:30 AM—30 Sep 2016

Donald Trump may be a bad president and a terrible human
being, but he's an outstanding mean girl.

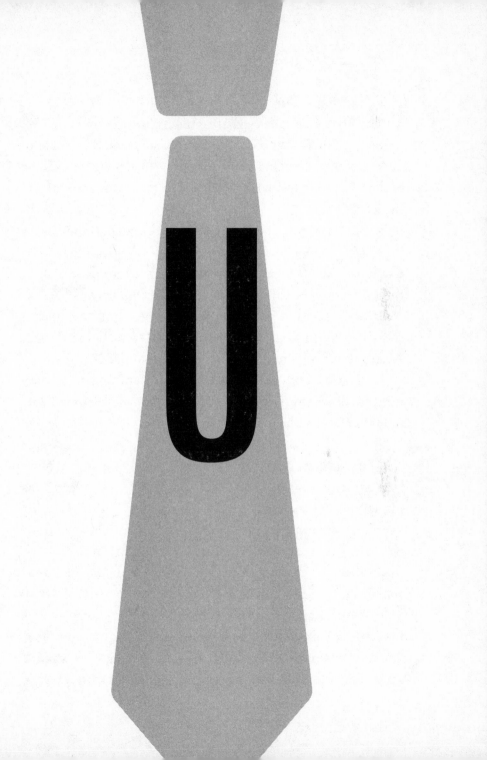

U is for Ubiquitous. Donald Trump is like Starbucks or the Zika virus—he's everywhere. Radio, press, Internet, TV— no matter where you go, there he is. I was watching a rerun of *Baywatch* last week, and I swear I saw him flouncing up the beach in a red Speedo, being chased by Pamela Anderson and the Hoff.

For all Trump's complaining about the media, they cover him 24/7. If he so much as burps, MSNBC breaks into its coverage of *Lockup* to bring us "Breaking News: Trump Belches in Bethesda." First of all, *not* everything Trump does is "breaking news." His saying or doing something stupid, disruptive, selfish, or damaging isn't even news; it's Trump being Trump. Breaking news should be saved for when he does something right, or smart, or in the best interest of someone other than himself. Since that's never going to happen, maybe Brian Williams can just make it up.

U is for Uganda. Idi Amin Dada was a cruel dictator who forever tarnished the reputation of Uganda. (Yes, "Dada" was his actual real last name, and no, it's not related to the early twentieth-century art movement, and yes, that's what Hans and Fritz call their father when he tucks them in at night. FYI: Amin dropped his last name for professional, show-biz reasons, just like Cher, Adele, and Carrot Top.)

Idi Amin's eight-year presidency, from 1971 to 1979, was marked by corruption, nepotism, political repression, economic chaos, murder, and delusion. (He thought he was the king of Scotland.) Amin had multiple children with multiple wives and liked to mock other world leaders (Henry Kissinger, Queen Elizabeth, Leonid Brezhnev) with crazy telegrams. He was also rumored to be a cannibal. In a 2003 story by Riccardo Orizio of the *New York Times*, Amin was quoted as saying, "I don't like human flesh. It's too salty for me." Which means of course that he's tried it—and I'm sure it wasn't in one of Uganda's myriad five-star restaurants offering tasting menus; he probably just snacked on one of his enemies.

U is for **UUUUUUGE.** Trump doesn't mispronounce words because he's a student of etymology. He mispronounces them because e's a *uuuuuge orse's ass.*

Except for the murder and the cannibalism, does any of this sound frighteningly familiar? Replace telegrams with tweets, and what've we got? That's right, Donald Trump Dada. But if these parallels ring true, then the most upsetting thing in the preceding paragraph isn't the corruption or the nepotism or even the murder; it's the phrase "eight-year presidency." I don't know that I can survive that. And if not, I just hope I taste good with ketchup and a side of fries.

U is for **Unchristian.** In his first overseas trip since assuming office, Donald Trump made a speech in Saudi Arabia. He mentioned God no fewer than seven times in thirty-three minutes. I don't think he's mentioned God that many times in his seventy years on the planet, and that includes the five and a half times he was having sex. I guess he was trying to show his Arab "friends" that he was the voice of morality in the Western world. (He must've figured they didn't know of his anti-Islam slurs, or that he dissed the Pope in 2016.)

But he's not the voice of morality. I'll bet he breaks at least four of the Ten Commandments every morning before he's even had coffee. So, why does Trump keep mentioning God? Because one of his handlers told him to, that's why. They figure his Republican base will like it. I don't claim to be an expert on Christianity, but from what I gather, Jesus was a role model with Christian values who would never, ever, have made massive financial cuts to services for the poor, women, and children in *His* budget. That's just what Donald did.

U **is for Unpredictable**. You know who likes unpredictability? Poker players, mystery writers, and Ashton Kutcher. That's about it. The rest of the friggin' world is not so thrilled with it; foreign countries don't want to be punk'd. Stock markets, for example, which are the basis for our capitalist economy, hate instability. They like things nice and steady and calm, kind of like my cat Benito Pussolini once his kitty downers kick in.

Foreign governments like predictability; they like to know who are their allies and who are their enemies. Surviving in today's world is not a game of *Survivor*. Donald Trump prides himself on being unpredictable, though. And if he were sitting at a poker table at one of his casinos, that would be fine . . .

Oh, wait, I'm sorry. His casinos all closed or went bankrupt. I mean if he were sitting at a poker table at someone *else's* casinos, that would be fine, but not when he's sitting in the Oval Office or the Situation Room. When the nuclear button is at your disposal, I think "predictable" is way better than "quick-fingered." I feel much safer with my cat Benito than Trump. Maybe Melania can slip some kitty downers into his ice cream.

U is for Utah. When I think of Utah, like most Americans, I think of Donny and Marie, the Mormon Tabernacle Choir, and Mitt Romney's underpants. For the record, I like Donny and Marie, the choir sings great, and I've never seen Mitt's underpants. But what I (and the people of Utah) *should* be thinking about are the great national parks in the state: Zion National Park, Arches National Park, and Bryce Canyon National Park. These three parks, along with the Grand Canyon and Larry King, are some of the country's oldest treasures. The Donald wants to do away with a lot of the protections the parks have, so he can open them up for drilling. The last thing we need in Utah is more gas. If you think I'm kidding, spend half an hour listening to Orrin Hatch. Admittedly, I'm not the outdoorsy type; I don't whittle, or husk, or, God knows, hike—I need a Sherpa simply to get across Amsterdam Avenue on the Upper West Side of Manhattan—but just because I have a close relationship with my sofa doesn't mean we should let the oil companies own our parks. It's bad enough they own our Congress.

U **is for *Uuuuuuge*!** For some odd reason, Donald Trump doesn't pronounce the *h* in *huge*. He treats it like a silent letter and, instead, says, "uge." Everything he's going to do is going to be *uuuuge*. The wall, the economy, and Hillary's prison cell—they're all going to be *uuuuuge* . . .

There are some words in American English that employ a silent *h* at the front, like *herbs*. Other words have a silent *h* in the middle, like *shepherd*, which is just an elision. But Trump doesn't mispronounce words because he's a student of etymology. He mispronounces them because e's a *uuuuuge orse's ass*.

V is for Vatican. Even though I was raised Catholic, I don't know a lot about God or religion. I never went to Catholic school; I hated the uniforms. But I do know it's not a great idea to take on the Pope. After Pope Francis said, "A person who thinks only about building walls is not Christian," Trump responded, "For a religious leader to question a person's faith is disgraceful." Calling the Pope "disgraceful" may not send you directly to hell, but you are now on report that you dissed the man who has a direct line to God. Why would anyone risk pissing off a guy with those kinds of connections?

V is for Vladdy Baby. I'm very worried that because Trump idolizes Putin so much, next week we'll see The Donald half-naked riding a Shetland pony around Mar-a-Lago.

V is for Vegas. I would like to move the White House, Camp David, Trump Tower, and Mar-a-Lago to Las Vegas. Because what happens in Vegas stays in Vegas. And nothing would please me more than to have the Family Trump stay there—and never leave.

V is for Vegetable. Michelle Obama built a vegetable garden at the White House. Melania Trump is putting in a panic room.

V **is for Vetting.** "Vetting" is how Melania Trump pronounces *wedding*. She should know; her husband's had three "vettings." Vetting is also the process by which potential government employees are screened to make sure they're cleared for work. It's basically a very deep and thorough background check. Apparently, The Donald either didn't fully vet a lot of his people or he did and just didn't care that they had dicey backgrounds. For example, I don't imagine he spent much time vetting Ivanka—not because she's his daughter or because he has a crush on her, but because she makes money for the family, so therefore, she's A-OK to come on board! He must've vetted Steve Bannon, and it didn't bother him that Bannon ran a website for neo-Nazis. Which makes me wonder: how could he not have known that Michael Flynn, Paul Manafort, and Carter Page were in business with the Russians? After all, Trump himself is in business with Russians. (His son Hans said so.) I think the next "vetting" Melania attends will be between General Flynn and his cellmate, Sergei (or, as he's known on Grindr, "the Siberian Husky").

V **is for Vitriol.** Vitriol is defined as "abusive, corrosive language used to censure, place blame, or create ill-will," or, as I like to think of it, any Donald Trump speech. Saying that there is a problem with illegal immigration is a fair topic for conversation; calling Mexicans "rapists and thugs" is vitriolic speech, the main purpose of which is to place blame and create animosity. If what's being said is true, sometimes the vitriol is well deserved. For example, referring to the 9/11 attackers as "monsters" or calling the guy at next table who's eating egg salad with his mouth open "disgusting" is harsh but nonetheless true. But Trump spits out venomous statements that are either patently false or aimed at people who don't deserve it.

Trump once said that "Arianna Huffington is unattractive, both inside and out. I fully understand why her former husband left her for a man—he made a good decision."

Did Arianna deserve that? Did she, in fact, turn her ex-husband gay? I doubt that, because if that were possible (to actually affect someone's sexual orientation), then all three of Donald Trump's wives, ex and current, would be lesbians. So, what was accomplished with Trump's vitriol? Arianna is still cute, her ex-husband is still gay, and Trump is still an asshole. Yes, I'm being vitriolic, but not only does he deserve it, but it is patently true.

V is for Vladdy Baby. You didn't think I'd forget Putin, did you? Yes, I've mentioned him in other chapters, but given the breadth of his power, the scope of his influence, and his cuckolding of Donald Trump, he could be in every chapter. Even though Putin was "elected" president of Russia, he's a dictator. He "governs" with an iron fist. He's been linked to murder, mayhem, and chaos all over the world. He started the war in Chechnya, he invaded the Ukraine, he annexed Crimea, and he's supporting Assad's reign of terror in Syria. Journalists have vanished, minorities and the media are tormented, and political opponents have mysteriously died. (And that's just a Thursday!)

Trump thinks Putin's a "strong leader." No. My husband's mother—let's call her Pearl—was a strong leader. She ran a mah-jongg game every week in the Bronx and conducted cha-cha lessons in her basement. If you so much as dropped a tile or missed a step, you were banished from the neighborhood for a week, sent home with a piece of kugel until you were eventually welcomed back with open arms and some ruggelah. Pearl was a leader; Putin is a menace.

Another thing that annoys me is that Putin's always photographed riding horses shirtless. In every picture, there's Vlad, sitting high in the saddle on Flicka, nipples ahead. Do I need to see this? Do the horses need to see this? My father loved to go to Belmont or Aqueduct to play the ponies almost every day. And not once, even in the middle of August, did he go topless. Nor did the jockeys, who, by the way, wear silk, a fabric not known for breathing. Maybe Putin thinks horseback riding makes him look macho, like a cowboy. But without the shirt, he looks like he's in an equestrian porn movie. I'm very worried that because Trump idolizes Putin so much, next week we'll see The Donald half-naked riding a Shetland pony around Mar-a-Lago. Haven't we suffered enough?

V is for Voir Dire: I'm an aficionado of TV crime shows. I know more about the court system than the judges do (in the way Trump knows more about ISIS than the generals do).

Which brings me voir dire, the jury selection process in which the opposing lawyers come up with twelve jurors they can agree upon. In theory, this should work, but in practice, it's not so easy. Let's say, hypothetically, that after Donald Trump is impeached, he is charged with various crimes (i.e., obstruction of justice, collusion, treason, ruining the ozone layer with too much hair spray) and goes on trial. In the United States, defendants are supposed to be tried by a jury of their "peers." In Trump's case, coming up with peers will be almost impossible. Where are we going to find twelve narcissistic millionaires with glued-down hair and orange complexions worthy of a Smucker's marmalade jar who only worship tax cuts? They don't exist—oh wait, they do: some of Trump's Cabinet and others in the Republican Party. Except for the hair and complexion, there is no dearth of Trump clones. He *would* get trial by a jury of his peers.

W is for W. Up until November 8, 2016, W. held the title of Least-Informed Person Ever to Become President of the United States. Now he's the Least-Informed Person Ever to Become Ex-President of the United States. Hopefully, he'll lose that title to Donald Trump, too.

W is for Walla Walla. The Washington State Penitentiary at Walla Walla is a maximum-security prison that would be perfect for Trump: it's got more than fifteen hundred rooms, it's fully staffed, three meals a day, and we, the taxpayers, would pay for his time there. Think of it as the Western White House!

W is for Walls. What's up with Republicans and their obsession with walls? They want to either tear them down or put them up. All day long, they're carrying on: "We're going to build this wall; we're going to tear down that wall; we're going to paint this wall; we're going to redo that wall; we're going to make this one out of brick and that one out of wood . . ." There are already plenty of famous walls: the Berlin Wall, the Great Wall of China, Hadrian's Wall, the Walls of Babylon. The world is wall to wall walls. But those walls are not enough for Trump and his supporters.

Trump is obsessed with building a wall between the United States and Mexico to keep illegal immigrants out. The fact that most people fly in from Mexico is an inconvenient fact. If Trump really wants to keep people out, he needs to build a forty-thousand-foot-high wall.

W **is for War.** George W. Bush started a war in Iraq and a war in Afghanistan; George Bush Sr. waged a war in Kuwait; and Ronald Reagan waged war on the island of Grenada, which is known as "the Island of Spice," famous for nutmeg. In his first hundred days in office, Donald Trump sent missiles into Syria, dropped a mega-bomb on Afghanistan, and threatened North Korea.

This has to stop. The Ancient Greek women had a solution. *Lysistrata* is a Greek play about women who withhold sex from their men until the men stop fighting the Peloponnesian War and negotiate a peace settlement. Works like a charm. The women cut off sex, and faster than you can say, "Not tonight, Pericles, I have a headache," the war is over and both peace and piece are at hand.

While I'm on the subject of war, what's with the "war on Christmas"? How seriously do right-wingers take the phony, nonexistent war on Christmas? In 2013, then-Fox anchor Megyn Kelly stated as a fact, "Everyone knows Santa is white." Kelly's GOP audience gave her full-throated support, ignoring the fact that Santa Claus is a fictitious character and not a real human being. (Don't tell the kids.) They even ignored the fact that he might have been at least half Jewish—Blitzen was actually his third cousin on his mother's side—and had a time-share in Boca Raton.

But the real war is the war on women. When it comes to women, Republicans are living in the past. For comedy's sake, I was going to be specific and say they're living in 1953, but that would imply that Republicans are okay with women having the right to vote (which we didn't get until 1920), and I'm not sure they are. I'll bet the GOP would overturn the Nineteenth Amendment if they could, just like they're trying to overturn *Roe v. Wade* and the Lilly Ledbetter Fair Pay Act, along with the paid maternity provision in the Affordable Care Act. If these conservative men (and some women) had their way, we women would be home, in the kitchen, wearing nothing but Saran Wrap, waiting eagerly for our man to come home so we could serve him a piping hot meal and tell him how wonderful he is. BTW, Saran Wrap causes excessive sweating, so this would work only until the onset of menopause.

W is for Waterboarding. Waterboarding is torture, and Candidate Trump promised he would do far worse than waterboarding. What could be worse than waterboarding? Well . . .

- Giving Mitch McConnell a sponge bath;
- Singing Yiddish karaoke songs with Henry Kissinger;
- Having Ann Coulter speak at a Black Lives Matter meeting;
- Taking Tiny Hands shopping for gloves; or
- Double-dating with Newt and Calista.

W is for Watergate. Watergate was the original "gate" scandal. It preceded Irangate, Contragate, Iraqgate, Monicagate, Bridgegate, Benghazigate, and Parsippanygate. (I'm not sure there was a Parsippanygate, but given that the media have dubbed everything "gate," what are the odds there wasn't a scandal in Parsippany at some point in time?) What I am sure of is that we are in the midst of Trumpgate—unless the media decide to call it Russiagate or Manafortgate or Flynngate.

Watergate and Trumpgate were both created by the same thing: Republican paranoia. Richard "I Am Not a Crook" Nixon was going to win reelection in 1972 by a landslide, yet his minions insisted on burglarizing the Democratic National Committee headquarters in the Watergate complex anyway. This led to the famous question "What did the president know and when did he know it?" As information began leaking, Tricky Dick tried to cover the whole thing up. Eventually, he resigned before being impeached, and Gerald Ford pardoned him so he wouldn't have to go to jail.

Fast-forward to 2017: Donald Trump's team may have been complicit in Russia hacking into the DNC computers. Once again, the question "What did the president know and when did he know it?" is being asked. What will the Trumpgate investigations turn up? Will Trump be impeached? Will he resign? Will he go to jail?

Will we have to think of his time away in prison as Walla Wallagate?

W is for **WikiLeaks**. Up until Trump's campaign, I thought WikiLeaks was an adult diaper.

W is for White People. I'm tired of hearing about the frustrated, angry white people who voted for Donald Trump. Day after day, it's the same thing: "frustrated, angry white voters, blahblahblahblahblah . . ." Look, I'm white and I'm frustrated. And I'm angry. I'm frustrated and angry that Trump conned so many white people into voting for him. But I'm not a complainer; I'm a problem-solver. (Think of me as an Italian Siri.) I have a solution. I think it's time to follow a simple rule: No white people after Labor Day. Basically, they're allowed to come out in the summer and go to the beach to turn brown. And then they're allowed back out.

W is for Why the Fuck Are We Paying for Trips to Mar-a-Lago? Between the White House and Camp David, we, the American people, have paid for two perfectly lovely homes for the president and his family. They are completely furnished, fully staffed, and have free Wi-Fi, ample parking, no noisy neighbors, regular trash pickup, and a full-time doorman. So, if Trump wants to schlep to Mar-a-Lago every weekend, why isn't *he* paying for it? He can't stop telling us how rich he is. Let him open his damned wallet. Not only do we have to pay for the White House and Camp David, but because Melania stayed so long in New York with the kid, we had to pay for that, too. Why should it cost the taxpayers a million bucks a day because she doesn't want to sleep with her husband? She's the one who said, "I do," so when the thirty-million-dollar monthly security bill comes in and she asks, "Who vill pay dis?" the answer is "You vill."

W is for **WikiLeaks.** Up until Trump's campaign, I thought WikiLeaks was an adult diaper. At rally after rally, Trump kept yelling, "Isn't WikiLeaks great? Don't we love WikiLeaks?" And, at the time, he did, because they were leaking secret information about Hillary Clinton and the DNC. He also had nice things to say about WikiLeaks's founder, Julian Assange, but that doesn't surprise me. Assange is wanted on rape charges back in Sweden. But now that WikiLeaks is leaking info on the Trump campaign's and administration's possible Russia connections, The Donald wants to break up with them. In fact, Jeff Sessions says leakers should be put in prison, and I hear that the Justice Department is preparing charges against Assange. I also hear that Trump was so upset he wet himself. Maybe I should go to the drugstore and buy him some extra-absorbent WikiLeaks.

W is for **Willie Nelson.** I don't know much about country music, but I love Willie Nelson. Any man willing to wear pigtails outside the house is a man I'd like to know. He's like a country-western Pippi Longstocking. And he's found the perfect way to deal with life in Trump World: Ever been on his tour bus? You can get a contact high just driving near it on the freeway. I think I might try to hitch a ride.

W is for **Wiretap.** Barack Obama didn't wiretap Trump's apartment any more than Kellyanne Conway's "microwave" spied on Melania vacuuming the hallway. Our intelligence agencies routinely monitor communications between noted Russian and

American officials and leaders. If you don't want to get caught communicating with Russia, don't communicate with Russia. The only wire I care about is the underwire in my bra.

W **is for Wolf Blitzer.** For years, Wolf Blitzer has been the face of CNN. (Sean Hannity and Tucker Carlson are the boobs of Fox.) Wolf Blitzer is a world-famous, well-respected journalist—respected by everyone, that is, except Donald J. Trump.

CNN has become one of Trump's favorite targets as an alleged purveyor of fake news. He probably goes after CNN more than most of the other networks because (a) they're an international news organization with a worldwide audience; (b) unlike Fox, they tell the truth; and (c) unlike Fox, none of their big names is a known sexual predator. I don't care if Trump goes after other news anchors, like Scott Pelley or Lester Holt or that young cute one with the nice hair on ABC, but leave my Wolfie alone! Not that Wolf needs me to come to his aid; he can handle himself. Last April, after it was revealed that Syrian president Assad was gassing his own people, Sean Spicer took his foot out of his mouth long enough to jam his entire leg in there when he said, "Even Hitler didn't use chemical weapons on his own people." And he said this during the week of Passover. Realizing the error of his ways—and by that, I mean Jared Kushner pulled him aside and said, "Dude! What the fuck?"—Sean went on CNN with Wolf to (a) clarify his incredibly ignorant remark; (b) make a broad, tepid apology, and (c) try to walk it back so he wouldn't lose his job. Wolf would have none of it because (a) it was the right thing to do; (b) his parents are Holocaust survivors, and (c) he's Wolf Fucking Blitzer.

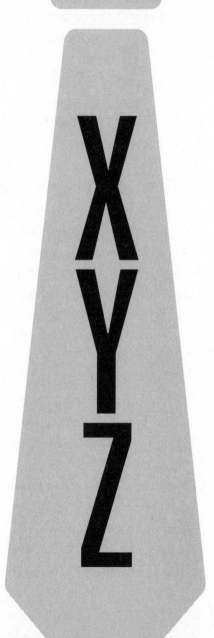

X is for Xenophobia. Some people probably (a) think this word is spelled with a *z*; (b) have no idea what it means; or (c) think it means having an irrational fear of Xena, Warrior Princess. For the record, the medical definition of *xenophobia* is "fear and hatred of strangers or foreigners or anything that is strange or foreign." Learning this was helpful to me, because I always thought phobias were just about fear, and that hatred was something else. Turns out they go together, like John Boehner and a shot of bourbon. For example, Mike Pence is homophobic—he both fears *and* hates homosexuals. I don't know what he's afraid of—that he'll wake up one morning and have an incredible urge to dump the wife and join the road company of *Hello, Dolly!*? And the argument that religious zealots like Pence use to justify homophobia, "Hate the sin, love the sinner," is a bunch of crap. Would they say the same thing about Jeffrey Dahmer, "Hate the butchery, love the cuisine"?

I don't think Trump is afraid of foreigners. Maybe he just hates them. Fine. Let him hate whomever he wants. The problem is he uses that hatred to instill fear in others. Yet, according to CNN and Homeland Security News Wire, between 2001 and 2014, a total of 3,412 Americans were killed by terrorists (including those killed on 9/11), while 440,095 Americans were killed by handguns. In the year 2014, only 32 Americans were killed by terrorists, while 33,599 were killed by handguns. Technically, Trump should be more afraid of guns than terrorists. And Pence should be more afraid of guns than gays.

XYZ is for XYZ. When I was in elementary school, if one of the boys accidentally had his fly open, all of us kids would yell, "*X-Y-Z, examine your zipper!*" As an adult, I still find myself saying this . . . every time I see Bill O'Reilly or Bill Cosby or Bill Clinton. Which makes me wonder, is there something about the name "Bill" that makes these guys want to free Willy? Does this mean that other men named Bill are going to waltz around flashing their bits? Will I find out that Bill Kristol leans to the right in more than just his politics? You might ask what this has to do with the Great Gasbag. Nothing, really, except that everytime he opens his mouth, I want to say, "Donald, *X-Y-Z, examine your xenophobia!*"

Y is for Sally Yates. Mother Teresa spent years and years washing the feet of the poor, until people took notice and said, "You know something, that Terry woman from Calcutta's a good egg." Sally Yates was acting attorney general for less than a month, but in that amount of time, she managed to become a hero to a lot of Americans. Because, unlike Paul Ryan or Mitch McConnell or most of the members of Congress with "(R)" after their names, she had the cojones to stand up to Donald Trump. Twice.

First came the Mike Flynn situation. Trump had named

him head of national security. As AAG, Yates went to the White House to give The Donald a heads-up about the general's Russian connections and possible vulnerability to blackmail. She went back once more to reinforce her warning. Obviously, she was ignored. And obviously, Trump wasn't happy.

Then The Donald issued his "travel ban," which was in actuality nothing more than a ban on Muslims, which Sally Yates would not enforce because it was unconstitutional. So, Trump did what any self-respecting seven-year-old would do: he fired Yates and then blamed and shamed her. The White House said she had "betrayed the Justice Department," and then Trump tweeted an unsubstantiated accusation that she'd leaked classified information to the press. FYI: since the time of her firing, Trump has rewritten the ban a few different times, and as of this writing, every single court it has come in front of has shot it down. Except the Supreme Court which allowed parts of the travel ban to take effect until they can hear all the arguments.

I don't know what Sally's plans are for the future—I've invited her to join me for my weekly mani-pedis; so far, no answer—but wouldn't it be fun to watch her run against Trump in 2020? And if not, even though she's not Catholic, maybe canonization? If Mother Teresa became a saint for caring for the homeless, surely Sally Yates should get something for standing up to Presidente Stoonad (Sicilian for "dummkopf").

Y is for Yentl. I was channel-surfing the other night, and on one of the networks the movie *Yentl* was playing. There was Barbra Streisand singing, "Papa Can You Hear Me?" and I'm thinking, *No, Barbra, he can't; the man's dead. Why don't you sing something from* Funny Girl? *It's much peppier.* And while watching *Yentl*, I realized that this movie is Republicans' worst nightmare. It's the story of a Jewish girl from a single-parent home who dresses like a Jewish boy so she can get an education and get ahead. Think about it: Jews. Cross-dressing. Empowered women. It'll drive them nuts. Plus, Barbra's a big liberal Democrat. As I write this, I'm planning a movie night. I'm going to invite Steve Bannon, Mike Pence, and Hans and Fritz over to watch *Yentl*. And as a surprise, I'm going to have RuPaul swing by with some kreplach. I can't wait! Barbra, can you hear me?

Y is for Yoko Ono. For years, Yoko Ono was one of the most disliked women in the country because everyone thought she'd broken up the Beatles. After John Lennon was killed, sentiments changed, however, and she became a sympathetic figure. But then she started "singing," and people started hating her again. But that was back in the '80s. Here in the 2000s, Yoko's place atop the Leader Board of Loathing has been taken by Laura Ingraham, who is doing her best to break up the country. The only good thing is that, to the best of my knowledge, Laura Ingraham doesn't sing.

Z is for Zzzzzz. The Lunesta I took three chapters ago is kicking in. I'm getting drowsy now. Wake me in four years when this nightmare is over. Wait a minute. No way Trump is going to last four years. Wake me in a few months; it'll be time to start writing the sequel.

Acknowledgments

There are many people I'd like to acknowledge for all the help they gave me in putting this book together, but I just don't have the time; I'm going shopping.

About the Author

JOY BEHAR is one of the co-hosts of ABC's hit daytime show *The View*. A former schoolteacher, Joy is also a legendary stand-up comedian. She has hosted several of her own TV shows *(The Joy Behar Show; Joy Behar: Say Anything!)*, and has written a number of books, including *Joy Shtick* and *When You Need a Lift*.